A Winter Walk

A Winter Walk

TOLBERT McCARROLL

With illustrations by Dorothy Beebee

May all your walks be blessed!
Tolbert McCarroll

A Crossroad Book
The Crossroad Publishing Company
New York

The Crossroad Publishing Company
16 Penn Plaza – 481 Eighth Avenue, Suite 1550
New York, NY 10001

Printed in the United States of America

The text of this book is set in 12/15 Venetian 301 Demi.
The display faces are Castellar, OptiAmadeus, and Trade Gothic.

Library of Congress Cataloging-in-Publication Data

McCarroll, Tolbert.
    A winter walk / Tolbert McCarroll ; with Illustrations by Dorothy Beebee.
        p. cm.
    Includes bibliographical references.
    ISBN-13: 978-0-8245-2416-6 (hardcover)
    ISBN-10: 0-8245-2416-0 (hardcover)
        1. Winter – Religious aspects. 2. Seasons – Religious aspects.
    3. Nature – Religious aspects. 4. Spirituality.   I. Title.
    BL590.M42 2006
    242 – dc22

                                                        2006013663

1 2 3 4 5 6 7 8 9 10   12 11 10 09 08 07 06

For my family, in love
and in gratitude
for walking through life
with each of them.

CONTENTS

PROLOGUE

ONLY IN WINTER can we see the full moon through the bare branches of a tree or hear the call of unseen geese piercing the cold night air. This is a season beyond our control — even with thermostats on the wall and frozen strawberries from the supermarket on the table. The earth has tilted. The sun is low. The days are short.

A nineteenth-century farmer referred to winter as "our season" because daily life was not dictated by when to plant or harvest. That person was probably born in a room with the ubiquitous sampler on the wall, which announced "To everything there is a season." And there was. It may not seem so today. Working in a cubicle on the tenth floor of an office building, we may find December 15 to be pretty much the same as July 15. Even so, winter is our season. The rest of the sentence quoted on that old sampler reads "a time to every purpose under heaven" (Ecclesiastes 3:1). What is winter's "purpose"? That is what we want to explore together.

We have all experienced times and places where we encountered something transcendent. Ancient Celtic peoples referred to these experiences as "thin places" where two parallel worlds come together. They had in mind mystic islands, like Iona. Certainly I have felt in uncharted space when on a mountaintop, at a Holocaust memorial, in St. Francis's Assisi, listening to Beethoven's music, at a time of birth or death. However, I think we also build walls around ourselves with our cares, our schemes, our preoccupations. If we are mindful, as the Buddhists would put it, we can find "thin places" in those walls where, like the

Celts, we discover there doesn't have to be much difference between the sacred and the ordinary. In the cycle of the seasons,
winter is the "thin place."

Countless people on many differing spiritual paths, and on
none at all, have made a pilgrimage of winter. I was born into a
Catholic tradition where this annual journey was spelled out in
the days of Advent. Something of that practice is undoubtedly
reflected both in my present life and in this exploration. Buddhists and Quakers, from whom I have learned much, might go
right to the quiet center of winter. But I need to move in little
steps. A story is told of a Russian Jew sentenced to the Gulag.
He thought he could sneak in one sacred book and asked his
rabbi what it should be. "The calendar" was the rabbi's imme-
diate response. True or not, there is great wisdom in that tale.
It is in the cycles of the year that many of us find our spiritual
paths — not in the doctrines or dogmas of religious institutions. This book is my invitation from someone who has tried,
for seventy-five years, to make reflective winter pilgrimages, to
heal, to prepare, to exult, to love. The experiences of many others
have enriched my own journeys. Some of these people have been
great thinkers. Most have been ordinary people who, often in a
humorous fashion, have enlightened my path. Smiles and tears
are part of being human, and of finding whatever we hold to be
sacred in our lives.

Many holidays, like Christmas, have a carnival atmosphere
that attempts to deny the authentic reality of our existence. But
a celebration need not be a time to fabricate our relations with
others or trivialize what is holy to us. Winter can be a unique
time of reflection and nourishment as we consider fundamental
issues against a background of festivals and the cycles of our
own lives. There are thirty-two essays in this book. I had in
mind reading only one a day. Of course you may choose to read

the book all at once, or backward. For those with a Christian heritage who wish to use the book as an Advent companion leading to Christmas and beyond, the fixed dates of some feasts are correlated with the number of the essay. I have assumed that most readers will spread out the reading a bit, and probably skip a few days, in the period between late autumn and early spring.

Thomas Merton observed that any contemplative writing must be largely autobiographical. My personal experiences of sharing the lives, and in some cases the deaths, of family and friends do seep in here. Some things are unique. There are not many whose father set fire to a neighbor's roof on Christmas Eve. But, even though some details come from happenings in my own life, I believe they usually reflect our universal experiences. There is also some personal quirkiness in these subjects that are dear to my heart. I think this is a necessary part of our being able to explore the wonders of a winter day. For example: my family lives on a farm, and brightly wrapped Christmas presents traditionally are found in the branches of orchard trees. When she was in kindergarten, my daughter, Holly, solemnly said to me, "Daddy, I don't think this is normal." Part of what fascinates me about this season is how we all do things differently while sensing our commonness.

This book appears at a time when, in some corners, our religious differences are being emphasized more than ever before in my lifetime. Nothing here is meant to be a part of that controversy. It is our common ground that I treasure. This book reflects a desire to deepen our response to life, not by ideology, which can so often separate us from each other, but by sharing the lived faith of each of us. That includes respecting a faith that may exclude religion as we commonly define it.

One of the dangers of a book like this is that what is intended as a mosaic ends up a tossed salad. There is a scheme here. I have tried to keep in mind the emotional steps many of us take at this time of year. If this book had a musical tempo marking, it would be andante — a walking pace. I have tried to modulate the rhythm and content of the sections. It starts in very accessible spaces between the secular and the sacred and, I hope, moves at times into deep places we have all traversed — or will.

My image for this book is a walk in which we visit friends, some of whom have differing experiences that may enrich us and broaden our horizons. We make this daily walk at a time of year that is often difficult because of the obligations, the frenzy, the triviality that accompany it, and for which our walk can be an antidote. In that emancipated frame of mind and heart, we may find something we hunger for, perhaps the breaking through of a divine spark in our ordinary life. There is nothing more to say. Read on and bring to life whatever is of value to you here.

Tolbert McCarroll
Starcross Community
Sonoma County, California

1

LEAVES

W INTER, ESPECIALLY LATE November and December, can be an arduous time of checking off items on a long list of things we "ought" to do. There can also be a tranquil truce in the wars we all fight in life. What makes the difference is usually something insignificant — like a falling leaf.

How does this work? Typically, for me, I am walking along, wrapped up in my preoccupations, when I become aware of a leaf floating down in front of me. To be honest, I am seventy-five years old and, at times, find letting go and drifting very appealing. As a result, my winter begins more often with a leaf on the sidewalk, than with a date on the calendar. For some time, leaves have been falling all around me, but then there is one I actually notice. It has happened on a country lane, a busy city street waiting for a light to change, outside a kitchen window, and once, incredibly, inside an abandoned thirteenth-century church atop a hill in Umbria.

Depending on where we were born or the spiritual path we walk, we will experience this time of year in different ways, but we all have similar longings. Like most people, I feel I am always toiling to keep things going right in the world or in my life. I worry about human misery, peace and justice, personal success, family responsibilities, and, occasionally, simply how to stay alive from day to day. Here is where the leaf enters. From nature's perspective, the falling leaf helps mark the end of a chapter for the tree that produced it. In our home orchard,

we have two pear trees. One, a Bosc, bears wonderful fruit.
The other, a Duchess, has never produced anything but really
terrible-tasting pears. At this time of year it doesn't matter. The
work of both is over. The trees will be bare for a while, and in
the spring new life will bring new leaves. Like the tree, can I
consider laying down my concerns for a time and accepting that
there are chapters in my life story? In medieval times truces
between hostile factions were often observed during this fallow
time. Can I stop warring with myself, with others, with the
circumstances of my life for a few weeks? If, like the leaf, I
come to rest and open myself to whatever is next, memories
flow. There have been so many times when love healed sorrow.

   December was always a special month for my mother. She had
known hard times, including keeping a family together during
the Great Depression and my father's long physical decline. For
her, Christmas was a time to put troubles aside and taste deeply

of the spiritual and secular nectar offered. As we entered the December when she was eighty-two, she had lost her sight and her reason was clouded. It was clear there was now a matter of days, not even months, before her life would end. It was also my son David's first Christmas. My emotions were pushed and pulled.

I found myself in a busy department store wondering what gift you get a person who is dying. It seems an inane question now, but it was very real at the time. I ended up with a package of "Christmas-scented" leaves. It was an unnerving experience, and I literally stumbled out of the store. It would be convenient to say a leaf fell from the sky, but it didn't. What did happen was that I dropped the package of leaves while waiting to cross the street, and someone stepped on it. I checked to see how much it was damaged. This was the first time I had really looked at the package. The leaves had obviously been dyed deep autumn colors. That sort of thing usually turns me off. But this time it was all right. They were still leaves. Clutching the cellophane package as if it were indispensable to my family's well-being, I went into a coffee shop and ordered a very strong coffee. I'm not fond of that stuff, but my mother, coming from southern Louisiana, loved it. The pungent aroma calmed me. I put the package of leaves opposite me on the little round table. Holding the warm cup, I recalled another difficult Christmas.

I was ten, which would have made it 1941, just a few days after the country went to war. We were living in an Oregon lumber town, and money was in short supply. I had become very tired of our poverty and ranted against it. I announced that we could not have a proper Christmas without a fireplace. All the magazine pictures showed families gathered around fireplaces, and most of my schoolmates had homes with fireplaces. My mother thought about what we could do. She put on her hat, and we walked down to Mr. Gerlach's drugstore. There, in the wrapping paper section, was a roll of brick-patterned paper she had remembered. We bought it and next went behind the grocery store, where we found a large box that had been discarded. We didn't say much on the way home or as we were cutting the box to look like a fireplace. But we were both very happy as we pasted the brick paper on the box. I had known my whining wouldn't produce a fireplace, but somehow we had transcended the issue by doing what we could. Years later we did have a brick fireplace, but that old cardboard replica was a treasured relic, sitting under the tree every year until it finally fell apart. It is strange how a common box became so important. Perhaps it had something to do with being satisfied with doing what we could. My response to my mother's last Christmas was clumsy, but I did what I could.

Picking up the battered packet of Christmas-scented leaves, I walked out of the coffee shop. My mother never smelled them. She died a few days later, and my son had his first Christmas. Somehow, it all worked out.

2

PLAIN AND SIMPLE

M Y SPIRITUAL LIFE probably would have been much more
stable had I been born into a Quaker, rather than a
Catholic, family. As it is, after three-quarters of a century and
much slamming and reopening of church doors, I have ended up
midway between the cathedral and the Friends' meetinghouse —
within sight of the local zendo.

If, on my religious journey, I had made it all the way down the
street to the Quakers, I would likely have some automatic inner
defenses against the commercialism and the stressful frenzy
of the holiday seasons. To start with, the seventeenth-century
Quaker founders did not think much of celebrating December 25 as the birthday of Jesus. They would speak of it as "the
time they call Christmas." Not only were there the issues that
no one knows the date Jesus actually was born and that much of
the festivities are of pagan origin connected to the time of the
winter solstice, but more important, there was the sense that the
birth of the inward-dwelling Jesus could be experienced every
time they sat in a silent meeting or indeed at any moment on
any day. One day could not be more holy than any other. Given
that point of view, and the Quaker abhorrence of all things fancy
and elaborate, it is understandable that their eventual tolerance
of Christmas was gradual and measured.

Contemporary Friends are able, if they choose, to use their
heritage to avoid much of the commercialism of the season.
How? Here is one example. After her children were born, my

friend Emily reflected long on her priorities at Christmas. She liked the simple beauty of outdoor lights on the Ohio snow; she saw no reason not to have a tree, to sing carols in the evening, or even give some simple gifts in the family. But as her children grew, she found that what she valued most was a time to relax and to visit. She freed herself from many distracting pursuits. Expensive gifts were not purchased. Cards were not sent out. Every room was not decorated with the latest bauble. Elaborate sweets were not prepared every day. The time she saved from not making lists, shopping in crowds, being a home decorator, and living in the kitchen was spent, she said, "in giving and receiving from others, and opening myself to the Light." Actually, she did make lists of a sort, but they were reminders to have more space than usual to be with her family and friends. She also planned to have more time for walks, silent prayer, and reading during December.

I think it is good to have at least one day a week when I exchange my guilt for Emily's guilt. I fret that my gift list is growing longer and I'm not crossing off many names. There is also a lot of "I should buy something for what's-his-name or he'll feel it is a slight." At the other end of the spectrum, Emily feels a bit guilty because she gave in to the younger grandchildren when they asked why they didn't have stockings on the mantle like "other kids." But she doesn't worry a whit about fulfilling social obligations with presents purchased at department stores or keeping up with the neighbors in outdoor displays. She does occasionally wonder how she would explain to her own Grandmother Lucy the string of colored lights on the fence and the tree next to the fireplace. What about following the suggestions in the newspaper for wondrous displays of Christmas decorations around the house? It never crosses Emily's mind, for she thinks perhaps she has already done too much.

Emily's Quaker guilt is a brake. My guilt moves me into a faster gear. I find it very refreshing to look about with Quaker eyes when I am using up my time with things I don't really want to do. I remember an unhurried and peaceful hour I spent beside Emily's fireplace the first Christmas after her husband died. It was there that she told me Grandmother Lucy would sometimes use the word "cumbrances," and the trick was to become free of them. That is a wonderful concept. I can imagine Grandmother Lucy observing a person in stress and saying, "Friend, perhaps thee has too many cumbrances." If I were that person, I would like to think I would try to shed at least some of them.

I find it freeing to act as if I am a Quaker for a Day from time to time and simply forget all the do's and don'ts of the season: the cumbrances. For a while, I can instead focus on the things that really are important to me and frame them in uncluttered time and space. Hopefully, in time it will all come naturally. But there is more to the Quaker faith than what they do not believe in or do. From my observances of Quaker homes in winter, the priority is to provide a space uncluttered by things or demands. This is where family and friends gather to share hopes and fears, pains and joys.

There can be nothing so beautiful or valuable as sitting with those we love, accepting each other as we are, and supporting each other toward a tranquil future. That is also what it means to be a winter Quaker for a Day.

3

STARS

O N A CLEAR WINTER NIGHT there is a simple way of feeling at home, and certainly not alone, in the universe. This comes naturally to many of the earth's first peoples.

Marti Aggeler, the practical visionary in my family, once referred to the inhabitants of the Kalahari Desert in a talk. She spoke of their almost exclusive focus on the simple fundamentals of existence — "first things." She was asked to give a personal example of "first things" for her. With tears in her eyes, she immediately responded, "I think of the stars. Living in a universe with the stars. Being a part of the same process and knowing it." She spoke those words in 1975, but I think few in her audience have forgotten that moment, which took us from an intellectual interest to a personal challenge.

Many indigenous people speak of listening to the stars, and some joke that the rest of us have to build giant radio antennae and dishes to hear what should come naturally in the quiet of the night. I consider myself fortunate to even be aware of the stars, let alone listen to them! Sometimes I wonder whether native peoples don't imagine these things, but at some level I know there is more to it. The Kalahari people talk of a specific sound, something like "tsau." The evasive desert animals are transfixed when they hear it, which allows the hunters to kill them for needed food. The hunters also hear the sound and understand it as a promise from the stars that the people of the Kalahari will survive. For them, listening to the stars is a process that

begins at birth. A new mother takes her child into the desert and prays that the great heart of a star be exchanged for her child's little heart. I believe that exchange is what Marti meant by living with the stars. It involves the courage to step into the future. Perhaps this happens more easily for those living in the desert.

Once a Hopi writer took me to a kiva on an Arizona mesa. This was a simple temple dug into the barren earth. He explained that the Hopi are traditionally a corn-based society. In the past, if there was no corn crop, the people starved. To guard against this, the seeds for the next year's crop are placed in the sacred space in the ground. An adolescent girl, herself a symbol of the future of the people, climbs down into the kiva and prays for several days in the darkness. Some adults stay aboveground, watching over her and also watching the stars. When the constellation we call Orion is overhead, the vigil ends. The trials of the winter are over, and a new chapter begins in the story of the people.

Stars, young people, seeds of the future. Perhaps this is what is behind the story in Matthew's gospel about the magi, scholars who interpreted dreams and signs in the heavens. According to the narrative, they were following a star because God, who seemed absent from recent history, was ready to embrace the whole human race in the person of Jesus. Like the Hopi, a new chapter was beginning for Matthew's people. At times this can be experienced in our individual stories.

When my son David was very young we went on "owl walks." We once accidentally spotted a great horned owl sitting on a telephone pole near our barn. It was a marvelous sight in the beam of our flashlight. After that wonderful night, we would occasionally go searching again. We seldom saw an owl. It was really the stars that held our attention. But because of the possibility of an owl, we spoke in whispers or not at all. These were times to value the cosmos and our relationship with it. As we looked at the vast universe, I could imagine David on a nocturnal vigil with his children long after my part of the story had ended. So there it was: stars, youth, the future.

One owl walk stands out in memory. David was four and at a "You know what?" stage. We had chosen a spot at the edge of an old orchard to wait for the owl and to gaze at the heavens. After a long silence, and still looking at the sky, David said, "You know what, Dad?"

"What?"

"Stars are flowers without stems."

At the time, David had a great interest in discovering small wildflowers, and I suppose this was a way for him to find commonness in his observations. For me it was different. The soil on which we stood was moist and covered with leaves from old fruit trees. Our feet made impressions in the ground, and it seemed quite natural for me to become conscious of the stems that bind me to the earth. Yet I longed to fly up among the stars. Standing next to a child calmly taking it all in, I truly seemed to hear the stars whispering in familiar voices. And I had no doubt that an exchange of hearts was in process. Something new was beginning with David, with both of us, and it involved the stars.

Perhaps it would be good to stop thinking about the stars, walk outside, and simply look up at the sky. Points of light in a dark sky do wondrous things to the human spirit. When it comes to sorting things out, there is hope and grace for each of us in just one still moment on a winter night. I doubt that any of us has completely forgotten how to listen to the stars.

4

RAMADAN

Some children I've seen in Oakland, California, begin the holiest month in the Islamic calendar by romping around the East Bay hills searching the sky for the first sliver of the new moon. When it is spotted, a very American yell goes up, followed by "Ramadan Mubarak" — may you have a blessed Ramadan. So much excitement from kids about a month of not eating or drinking between sunrise and sunset? They know there is a lot more to this month than fasting.

Muslims speak of *taqwa,* a consciousness of God, as the central theme of Ramadan. In the Oakland hills, that process of a heightened sense of the divine begins as the children focus all their attention on the moon. At first they see nothing in the sky; then the thin crescent of the moon appears. Any quest for the sacred is often that way. First comes only a brief glimpse of what we hope for. Is it real or not? Slowly our hope, like the moon, waxes.

Ramadan is not part of my cultural experience, but over the years I have listened appreciatively to those living within the Islamic tradition. I found I had many things to learn. The holy month can come at various times in the year, but I always associate it with the winter because that is when I first became aware of it.

Life during Ramadan is unlike existence in any other month. The family gets up before dawn and eats a big meal. There may be an omelet made of local farm-fresh eggs and desert dates cooked in butter. Who says you have to lose weight during Ramadan! Then the household prays and makes a pledge to fast from all food and drink (and smoking and sexual encounters as well) until sunset. The regulation is that only those who have reached puberty must fast. It surprises me how many younger children also choose to fast. When they leave the house, life becomes challenging for them. For non-Muslim students, school can be one long period of snacks, drinks, and lunch. It is hard to abstain. So why do it? Muslim kids are told the fast builds self-reliance. There is something of the desert about the whole experience. If we cannot fast, we will not survive in the desert. If we cannot learn to control our obsessions and distractions, we may not do well in life. Undoubtedly all that is true, but it can be a very long day for young people.

The family assembles as the sun sets. They sometimes eat a few dates and drink water, as the Prophet Muhammad did long ago in Arabia. There are evening prayers followed by a great joyful dinner. Later they go to the local mosque and pray with all the other families whose day has been similar. In the service they are encouraged to forgive others and ask forgiveness. During Ramadan there is to be no vulgarity or dishonesty of any kind. Natural reactions to personal slights are checked as people remember, "This is Ramadan." There must be kindness all the time, which includes feeding the hungry, those among us for whom every day is an involuntary fast day. There is a poem by Persian poet Sa'di (ca. 1200–ca. 1291) with the line "If you are not moved by the suffering of others you are not worthy of being called human." Muslims often use the mosque to channel charity to people in need nearby and across the oceans. There is a strong sense of community as those who have gathered for Ramadan prayers emerge from the mosque and into the moonlight.

Ramadan is geared to the moon that passes through its phases in the same way each person experiences the changes in his or her heart. Most Muslims study the Quran during Ramadan. One evening commemorates the night when the Quran was revealed to Muhammad in a cave. It is a very holy time, and some Muslims pray all through the night. When the last of the now-waning moon has disappeared, Ramadan is over and there is a great public feast.

All any one religion can do is present a facet of divine beauty that can never be fully comprehended by any single individual or faith community. We are all the heirs to the many religious traditions that have evolved on this planet. We can all respect, and learn from, each other's struggling. So what can non-Muslims take from the celebration of Ramadan? Perhaps the most important thing is to keep asking that question. It is the same question a non-Christian can ask about Christmas. A non-Jew about Chanukah. A non-Buddhist about Bodhi Day. A non-Hindu about Diwali. A non-European about St. Nicholas Eve or Santa Lucia Day. A non-Hispanic about Posadas. Muslim clerics might see my gleanings as trivializing their observance, just as many Christian clerics are adamant that God cannot break through in any culture but their own. But we are all humans stumbling along paths that we hope will bring enrichment to our lives, and it is good to share our journeys with each other. So what do we take from Ramadan?

Again, the moon is a safe place to start. If I want to watch the progression of time, I normally look at a wall calendar. It is good to briefly go back to those days when most people marked time by watching the phases of the moon. When I make a point of nightly moon watching, it is not hard to understand that there is something bigger than me going on in the universe. But what about the fasting? That is harder. Having been raised in the Catholic tradition, I was pressured to give up all manner of things for Lent in preparation for Easter. As a child, I never could see why my not going to the movies for forty days could possibly be of any interest to God. I'm sure a lot of Muslim kids have the same thought. "Is my not being able to have a drink of water after soccer practice really going to make Allah love me?" If I were a follower of Islam, I would now be ancient enough to be excused from the fast, but I would have to feed at least one hungry person for every day that I did not fast myself. Again comes the message that not only in the heavens but also on the earth, I am not the only one who counts. Perhaps that is even more strongly represented in the need to forgive and ask forgiveness, to avoid fighting and vulgarity, to be completely honest. What's the point? To get outside my preoccupation with myself and to make a better world. That is not hard to do for an hour on Sunday morning in church. But for a whole month? That is hard and also rewarding. What if I forget? That is where the fasting comes in. It is meant to keep the Muslim community focused on being the best they can be.

Ramadan is a very significant observance in this world. There are about a billion Muslims struggling to live their faith fully at this time. For the rest of us, it can be the sound of a distant bell encouraging us to remember the desert people and that there are times when we must all travel undistracted. For life can be a serious challenge.

It can also include eating a few dates in the moonlight.

5

ADVENT WREATH

OUR FAMILY SELLS thousands of evergreen wreaths every year. I like shipping them around the continent. To me the wreath, like any circle, is a symbol of unity — something we need more of at the moment.

Traveling down the highway, I saw two bumper stickers ahead of me: "Keep Christ in Christmas" and "Keep Religion in Church." I would like to tiptoe around the occupants of both those cars, but it is not so simple. Religion is an increasingly strident factor in our society. For most of my life, there was a vague consensus that church attendance was part of growing up and learning to be a good person. Most of the people I knew went to Christmas Eve services, if only for the music and the decorations. Respectable people were married, buried, and occasionally comforted by proper clergy. Although a few fanatics ranted in the backwaters, religion didn't really trouble most Christian Caucasians. Then, in the closing decades of the twentieth century things changed.

While Europe, our older spiritual sister, was clearly outgrowing church and creed, Americans began to take religious beliefs, pro and con, very seriously, as has happened several times before. The Great Awakening in colonial times was a widespread evangelical movement that renewed and redefined Christianity for many colonists. Existing church authority was questioned. This helped lay the foundation for questioning political authority and contributed to the American Revolution. However, it also

created great gaps between people of differing beliefs and practices, which took years to close. The Second Great Awakening of the early nineteenth century echoed the first. Now, in the twenty-first century, deep religious rifts are separating us again. Sometimes the only thing we share in common is the intensity of our feelings. Free-thinking-Buddhist-leaning grandparents find themselves facing born-again evangelical grandchildren over issues like saying grace before a holiday meal. On the other hand, their neighbors, lifelong churchgoers, are seeing their lawyer daughter and her partner married in a vineyard by a friend who was ordained online for the occasion. Conservative students at Ivy League schools are using the chapels for prayer meetings for the first time in many years. And some people are intent on making the United States a Christian theocracy. They are occasionally supported by troubled folks who see no other answer to the social problems in our society or among the youth of our nation.

I certainly don't know where we are as a people except that we are very divided and, as is our tendency, more concerned with what we say we believe than with how we live. This can create some interesting tensions at this time of year. What do we do because our beliefs require it and what do we reject because our beliefs require it? My poor barber wrote "Happy Holidays" on his shop window and found himself accused of attacking the Christian religion. A local fundamentalist minister urged his congregation not to trade at stores where they did not greet you with "Merry Christmas." Another minister condemned the use of "merry" as a sacrilege. I think it is important not to be distracted by these things, especially when the issues are personal.

Berkeley, possibly the most secular city in the Western hemisphere, is host to the University of California, which is in turn host to all manner of liberated people. Monica was one of those, a German exchange lecturer on avant-garde literature. She was a third-generation "church free" person. Monica was also the single mother of a young son. Which is why she asked a colleague, "Where in Berkeley can you buy an Advent wreath?" Her friend could not have been more perplexed about where to get such a superstitious thing or why Monica would want one. Realizing her shocked friend was still fighting a battle with the faith of her mother or grandmother, Monica let the subject drop. She ended up making her own wreath, with four candles to mark the weeks before Christmas, which is what her parents had done for many years before the growth of German Christmas markets made it easy to purchase such items. As parts of the world become more secular, it is interesting to see which cultural symbols of Christmas are retained. The wreath has fared rather well.

Advent means "coming." What's coming? For many, it is the celebration of the birth of Jesus. For children, it is the coming of St. Nicholas, Santa Claus, Father Christmas, Père Noel, Befana, the Three Kings. It can also be a time of increased of awareness, and even wonder. Advent practices can make people feel good, which is why Monica wanted to do this for her son, and perhaps for herself. She did not want her son to be religiously illiterate. Biblical stories, like Greek myths, form a powerful part of the references and foundations of modern literature. Yet she would never have considered sending him to a church or synagogue. So she used religious festivals as a time to relate biblical stories to him. There was another consideration. Having traversed an agnostic adolescence herself, Monica knew it could be rather arid, and it reduced Christmas to exclusively materialistic concerns — especially in America. Although Monica totally rejected all vertical aspects of religion, the relationship between God and people, she saw some value in the horizontal aspects, which emphasize the relationships between people. For her the cornerstone of the gospels was the story of the Samaritan taking care of a stranger in need (Luke 10:29–37). This was how she approached the use of an Advent wreath. It was through this practice that she first remembers her parents teaching her about the necessity of caring for each other and responding to those in need.

The ritual in Monica's childhood home was simple. Usually just before or after dinner, when everyone was at home, the family gathered around a wreath with four candles. The first week they lit one candle each evening, the next week two, and so on. The candles were named: Love, Hope, Joy, and Peace. The family sang, read, and shared dreams for themselves and for the world. It didn't trouble Monica's church-free parents that many people saw this as a Christian, usually Catholic, practice. They used the wreath ritual because it came from a cultural heritage that

belonged to them too. Besides, as her father was fond of pointing out, when you get right down to it, the Catholic Church
lifted the Advent wreath ritual from a pagan society.

The first evergreen wreath was probably a wagon wheel in
some northern European village. It had been brought in to protect it from winter weather. So what do you do with a big
wheel in the middle of your little house? As the days are getting
shorter and colder, you wonder whether the gods have forgotten
about you. So you decorate the wheel with evergreens, the only
growing things you can find, and put candles on it to simu-
late flowers. The big wreath is a reminder to the gods, and to
ourselves, that spring will come. And it will.

There are many variations on the Advent wreath. On the Sun-
days of December, each person in my family collects something
outside to put into a large wreath that we construct on a table.
Seeing some of the things the children bring, I occasionally
wonder about the outcome, but it is always beautiful, precisely
because of the diversity and the surprise. Sometimes we read a
poem or sing a song. We almost always speak of friends, family, and events. It is a time for sharing stories we have heard
about people facing challenges and to consider whether we could
help in some way. Each Sunday we add a candle to the wreath.
We light it in silence, and we know that we are doing something we will remember. Like the ring of the wreath itself, past,
present, and future become one experience for me. Standing
quietly, looking at the candle flame with those I love, it is the
unity between us that matters. Our shared past. Our support for
what lies ahead. The wreath has come to symbolize our common
roots as well as our diversity.

The religious feasts of winter only have spiritual meaning if
they are used to transcend our differences and help us form a
large human circle of love, hope, joy, and peace.

6

ST. NICHOLAS DAY

F OR THE PAST FEW YEARS, there have been letters on the Internet from agnostic Dutch college students defending the celebration of St. Nicholas Day. For Christians in the Netherlands, especially those in the tradition of the Dutch Reform Church, December 25 is a solemn day for church services and family dinners. But most Dutch people approach December 6, the Feast of St. Nicholas, with a very different attitude. Any attempt from either religious or secular fundamentalists to change tradition will be opposed. For this celebration is not about belief or non-belief, but about a faith in the capacity of people to find pleasure in each other and in their lives. We outside the Netherlands can learn something from how St. Nicholas Day is celebrated. It has to do with sharing our deep feelings about those we love.

Of all the characters associated with winter, few can equal St. Nicholas. His legend is probably mixed up with stories about the principal Norse god, Odin, who, like Nicholas, flew around on a great white horse and popped gifts down chimneys. But it really doesn't matter where it started. For a long time now, it has been all about St. Nicholas.

The Dutch are very tolerant of the St. Nicholas Day celebrations in the rest of Northern Europe, but they know full well that the real St. Nicholas, Sinterklass, lives in Spain, and he arrives at a Dutch seaport in mid-November with a big red book that he promptly opens in order to publicly discuss (these days

on national television) the misdeeds of the mayor's blushing
children. Sinterklass's little Moorish helper has been gathering
data on everyone's conduct all year; Odin had two ravens who
listened at chimneys. With that ritual of gentle confrontation,
the Sinterklass season begins. This little drama of Nicholas's
visit will be enacted in almost every household in the Netherlands, Christian and non-Christian alike, before December 6. It
is not just a celebration for small children. All ages revel in the
festivities.

Who was this fellow? Nicholas did exist. He was born
around 271 CE and was bishop of Myra in present-day Turkey.
Many legends of good deeds surround him. He secretly tossed
dowries for poor maidens down chimneys or through windows,
saved falsely imprisoned people, and delivered children from all
manner of harm. Somehow he even became the patron of pawn-
brokers. But what made him so popular in maritime-centered
Holland was that he befriended sailors, whom he protected from
storms and other disasters. At times Nicholas admonished the

rescued sailors to go and help others, and they were perhaps the first of what the Dutch now call *hulp-Sinterklazen* or "Helpers of St. Nicholas," a very worthy profession for anyone from teens to centenarians.

Despite all the excitement, the celebrations remain simple. Literally taking a leaf from St. Nicholas's big red book of human foibles, this is a time for gentle humor and teasing. There are gifts, but they are usually inexpensive and must be camouflaged in some way. Often a treasure hunt is involved. And a clever poem is always attached. The poem is anonymous and hints at some shortcoming of the recipient. The signature is always "Sinterklass," and the required response, no matter what one's age, is "Thank you, Sinterklass."

On the evening of December 5, everyone heads home. There are many traditional foods and often large chocolate letters, one for each person's first initial, serve as place cards at the table. A basket of presents, with poems attached, is the center of attention. Each person in turn must read out the poem tied to her or his gift, which is then opened to the pleasure of all. The emphasis is not on commercial value, but on creativity. I once delivered a St. Nicholas Day gift of chocolate to a chocoholic Scotswoman who had performed in the Netherlands Chamber Orchestra for a number of years before moving to California. Her instant response to my gift was, "Where's the poem?" That was what she truly prized. On the days before St. Nicholas Day, poems appear everywhere in the Netherlands — schools, offices, the media, churches, Parliament.

As we reach out to each other at this time of year, we could consider something like a St. Nicholas poem. But it is not easy. Many years ago I accepted a hulp-Sinterklazen role, in our very American home, of seeing that the stockings were filled on

Christmas Eve. Somehow I found the time to write to each person and, for me, this was the most important part of the job. I could be clever and impressive with the little gifts and treats, but the letter meant more than all the rest. As the years rolled on it seemed there was less and less time in December and the letters faded away. If I were to undertake them again, I would have to begin them long before December 24. There are so many questions that need time for reflection before I put my thoughts into a letter. What has the person faced this year? What have they contributed to others? How do I put into words my love for them? What has life been like because of them? And there are the memories that need to be shared. These often do not surface without a lot of quiet space. But they are essential. If there are tensions in our relationships, it is important to share memories of times when busyness and conflict didn't matter — only love did.

If individual Christmas letters are begun early they can grow and mature as the season goes through its phases. The sixth of December, St. Nicholas Day, seems a good time to begin the process.

7

SLOW TIME

S OME OF MY CHILDHOOD MEMORIES of winter nights are very
dark and prolonged. None were more snail-like than those
when I was seven and seated with my family on the sleeping
porch of my Aunt Net's Mississippi home. In the days before
air-conditioning, large homes in the South had screened-in areas
for more comfortable sleeping during the summer. The porches
were rarely visited in winter.

My aunt was not given to occult practices. She was an Epis-
copalian and married to John Wesley Reed, whose mother was a
stern and ranking official in the Methodist church. Yet here we
sat, night after night, in the winter, about twelve of us, shivering
in complete darkness, staring intensely in the direction of a tall
flower stalk in a ten-inch clay pot.

The plant on which we focused was a large, and supposedly
rare, lily. Aunt Net had obtained the bulb from a traveling salesman the previous summer. It only bloomed once every century,
claimed a teenaged cousin. My Uncle John thought it might
bloom every other year. From my point of view, the evenings
seemed to last forever. I usually fell asleep in my mother's arms.
My father never joined us, having the excuse that he had an early
shift at the lumber mill.

It was faith alone that motivated my aunt to watch for that
bloom. She *knew* what was going to happen. The lily would open
at midnight on Christmas Eve and inside, the pistil and stamen
would be shaped so as to form a crèche. The original of this

species, claimed the traveling salesman, bloomed in the fields at Bethlehem on the first Christmas Eve. Because of time zones and the like, my aunt thought we best be prepared for an earlier opening. Most of our county might be asleep, but Aunt Net was determined that her family would be alert when the lily revealed its secret. One long evening followed another. At some point my irreverent bachelor Uncle Richard whispered to me, "I think the damn thing's dead!" Still we remained faithful.

The flower did not open by December 24, but it did unfold on the afternoon of the twenty-fifth. Uncle Richard had gone out on the sleeping porch to sneak a smoke after Christmas dinner. Excitedly he raced in to report a small opening at the end of the bloom. My aunt picked up a long silver flashlight like a scepter, and we all followed her out to the porch.

By nightfall the bloom had opened enough for each of us to peek inside. Aunt Net held the flashlight at the back of the flower. The light filtered through the petals and illuminated the interior in a pleasant way. Most of us had trouble seeing anything revealed other than the normal parts of a flower. My aunt, who clearly saw the Holy Family, decided to awaken our faith by reading the Christmas story from St. Luke's gospel. When it became evident that no one was leaving that sleeping porch until our eyes had been opened, we all converted and then were allowed back into the house for some of my mother's fruitcake.

Looking back, I have to admit there were some interesting things about those vigils. The strange sounds of the night fascinated me, as did the unfamiliar constellations of bright stars beyond the silhouettes of the adults. It was also a new experience to be with my relatives when they were not all talking at once. And there was something more.

Like any child, I was very excited about the coming of Christmas. There were many activities at school and in the town. All of these came to a halt in the evening when we went to the sleeping porch. In the process, I became open to having several contrasting themes in my winter days. The time on the sleeping porch that year increased my awareness of the other facets of Christmas. Much later in my life, I discovered that orchestral music usually has a slow movement between faster sections. These sections are often marked "adagio," which means "at ease." The slow pace helps us be more conscious of the sparkle and vigor of the movements on either side.

Contemporary life, and most individual lives, continually moves at a rapid pace. There is not much in our culture that encourages us to slow down. In general our youth today live at a faster clip than did their parents. The entertainment industry has learned, or perhaps taught, that there must be no spaces between actions. It was not always so. When storytellers provided much of the education and entertainment for hunting tribes, sagas shared around the evening fire would often intentionally open slowly. Listeners and learners must, at times, be at ease. Hunting tribes knew that youth must learn patience if they were to be successful hunters. So must those of us making a winter pilgrimage.

I have now surpassed the age of the aunts and uncles with whom I sat on those cold nights. And I have come to wonder whether nocturnal quests are not a necessary part of my Christmas preparation. How many times have I walked quietly with friends looking at the night sky or rocked sleepy children in a room lit only by a Christmas tree? Every one of those experiences has helped me find the divine in the darkness, and appreciate the slower beat of my heart.

And it all began while sitting on a dark porch waiting for a lily to open.

8

BODHI DAY

Tucked between two glamorous and expensive San Francisco neighborhoods are a few streets with aging Victorian houses. I would not describe them as quiet streets because they are home to many children. When school lets out, there is a riot of diversity in ethnicity and dress. But there is also a unity among the kids, which reflects the streets themselves. Most of the flats have bay windows and this time of year there are lights in almost every window. Though some of the trees bearing lights are evergreen Christmas trees, some are dwarf fig trees, known to Buddhists as "Bodhi trees." The trees may differ, but the strings of lights decorating them all come from the same local hardware store and reflect what we all hold in common. Both the evergreen trees and the fig trees are symbols of the aspirations of the people who live behind those windows.

How much can we authentically share in a culture that differs from the one in which our parents raised us? Let's think about these San Francisco school kids. Who are their ancestors? Is Mahatma Gandhi as real to those students whose grandparents came from India as the American Civil Rights leaders they spoke of in class today? For young people it usually works out somehow. Anyone, from any culture, who struggles with the fundamentals of existence helps lay a foundation for all of us.

One ancient and towering relative of those little fig trees in the bay windows was the tree where Siddhartha sat down, resolved not to get up until his mind became clear about the nature of existence. He was a young man of twenty-nine and it was about six hundred years before the birth of Jesus. What happened to Siddhartha under that fig tree became known as enlightenment or Bodhi which is why the fig tree was thereafter called the Bodhi tree and the young man became known as the Buddha. December 8 is the day when many Buddhists celebrate this moment of enlightenment and decorate little fig trees.

For eight days Siddhartha confronted his inner demons: greed, self-doubt, anger, restlessness, hatred, violence. He understood that we all suffer because of craving what we want and running from what we fear. Either way, we ignore our own nature. In fundamentals, we have not changed much since Siddhartha's time. It came to him that we can be liberated from this sad state by comprehending the essential oneness of life. How do we do that? Life is a journey. On that adventure we must be careful to respect eight guideposts. Greatly oversimplified, the instructions go something like this: we must try to be free of delusion, prejudice and superstition; we must turn from any false values and hypocrisies even though they pervade our society; our conduct must always be peaceful and compassionate; our speech must not harm and must be kindly; our work must have no bad consequences; we must make a constant effort to avoid narrow-mindedness and overcome harmful desires; we must develop and cherish an awareness of the small acts of ordinary daily life; and we must regularly enter the nothingness of meditation. In this way we will comprehend the oneness of life and grow as a part of the universal Buddhahood. I have not often walked this path and should not attempt to go beyond this simple description. Nonetheless, December 8, Bodhi Day, seems a good time to focus on the priorities in our lives and to be more mindful of our actions and non-actions. What we learn about ourselves may often be hard to accept, but usually it is valuable to us.

At a recent conference in Oxford, an author asked whether his life was truly better because his supermarket had 175 different salad dressings or because he had learned to speed-read a bedtime story to his child. Unlimited choice and instant gratification are marks of our contemporary life. And, as far as the Buddha's suggestion of meditation, there are now courses on speed-meditation that claim to get the same results in just a few minutes. For all of us, it is the process, not the goal, which should matter. I was a cradle Catholic and until I hit college thought Buddha was a little statue that served as a holder for incense sticks. Nonetheless, what Buddha taught of his experience has something to do with my experience of life. And the most fundamental of all his teachings is, perhaps, meditation.

Breathing is something we have done all our lives. It is so simple that we are sometimes embarrassed to let it lead us into the quiet prayer of meditation. But it works. Now I am breathing in. Now I am breathing out. In. Out. In. Out. Hey, there is a whole peaceful nowness in here somewhere which encourages me to live. In this moment, the Christmas tree and the Bodhi tree don't seem very separate.

Someone told me that the lights strung on a Bodhi tree are always multicolored to demonstrate that there are many paths to spiritual liberation — enlightenment. Can there be any relationship between Jesus, whose birth we are soon to commemorate, and the Buddha's enlightenment? Vietnamese Zen master and peace activist Thich Nhat Hanh thinks so. In a Christmas Eve talk at his French spiritual center, Plum Village, he once called Jesus and Buddha brothers. He suggested that for anyone in the Western, European-based world Jesus was a spiritual ancestor. The same was true about Buddha for many people in Asia. We should be working toward a time when our own descendants have both Buddha and Jesus as spiritual ancestors. "If," he advised, "you need one hundred years to arrive at this position, it is very worthwhile." Our spiritual ancestors are a real part of us, they are in our makeup and can be called upon. As he said on that Christmas Eve: "Sometimes you are overwhelmed by the energy of hate, of anger, of despair. You forget that in you there are other kinds of energy that you can manifest also. If you know how to practice [meditate] you can bring back the energy of insight, to bring back the energy of love, of hope.... Our ancestors [Buddha and Jesus] are capable of negating the malignant spirit within us and bring back the holy spirit in order for us to heal and to be healthy and to be joyful, to be alive again."[1]

That's a pretty good agenda for this day. It is certainly worth finding a bench and sitting down for a while and doing nothing in order to become mindful of what it means to be alive again.

In. Out. In. Out.

Across the street, the Bodhi trees and the Christmas trees are showing off their multicolored lights, and it is very hard not to smile.

9

THE OLD NEIGHBORHOOD

Nostalgia usually takes a while to kick in. As I was finishing middle school, my main desire was to be liberated from the place where I grew up. Everything moved in slow motion as I slogged through the remaining years of school. My parents and teachers were nice, but I eagerly awaited the day when I could dash into the great outer world of opportunity and fulfillment. In my case, the old neighborhood was a little lumber town in Oregon. For others it might be a street in Manhattan. It doesn't matter.

As the years go by, we sometimes find ourselves buying Christmas cards with paintings of someone else's hometown or countryside. At some point it occurs to us to reexamine the experiences we had in our own hometown, be it Boston's Back Bay or Sonoma County's Dry Creek Valley. Why? These reflections can enrich and give roots to our present-day experiences. At times of winter dissatisfaction, I sometimes ask myself, "What do you want from this day anyway?" And that often translates to "What's missing?" which in turn takes me back to little things like frosty windows when I was young and had no obligations or obsessions except to bring in wood for the fire and read. Perhaps remembering earlier times helps us be more aware of enrichments that we tend to ignore. If for no other reason, those memories give us stories to tell the young.

As I recall winters long ago, my first layer of memory is often the weather. There was never snow and ice. It was sunshine in

Mississippi and rain in Oregon. Nonetheless there was a special nippiness. As I go deeper, little things become important: colors, sounds, smells. At some level I almost always hit on times when I had an extraordinary experience of something very ordinary. Most of us grow up being actors in life. That is why, I believe, we learn to value the times when we are not acting. Here is one such time from when I was living in Springfield, Oregon.

The rain had stopped early in the morning. Still in bed, I could hear the crackling of wood in the cookstove in the kitchen. Looking out the window, I saw a world that was neither bright nor dark. The year was 1941 and I was almost eleven. It was a few days after Pearl Harbor had been bombed, and I understood this would be unlike any other Christmas.

Springfield was a small lumber town in Western Oregon. My father was a grader at a local mill where most of the workers had come up from the deep South. This Saturday morning my job was to go to the grocery store and pick up the turkey, a gift from the mill owner. We never owned a car, and errands were often my task since Dad had made me a wagon. I started after breakfast — going on a walk in a town from which I already was longing to escape. Yet that walk is a very real part of me now, sixty-five years later.

I can see the earth, covered with brown leaves, a few still sparkling with frost. Some people have turned on their Christmas tree lights. Likely this is for the older teenaged boys who are leaving for the war. Families want as much of Christmas as possible. Even at this early hour there is visiting going on. My cousin Darwin is leaving for the Navy next week. As I pass his house, I notice my aunt has come out on the porch to cry. Putting down her blue handkerchief, she waves. Their tree lights are on.

From habit, I detour past my school. Pulling my wagon, I boldly enter the empty playground, where I usually feel more cautious. The school is a big wooden three-story building that has served many generations. It has been a good place for me. When I came to Oregon I was an alien. We were Southerners in a Western culture. To make matters worse, we were Catholics in a Protestant environment. Today no one is at the school. I look through the window into my classroom. So many things happened there, but what I remember vividly now, many years later, are the little pins with flags wrapped around them. Every morning we moved them around a world map as the war progressed. It was no game. They represented the places where fathers and older brothers were stationed and fighting.

Another few blocks and I am downtown. As always my first stop is the used bookstore where I discovered most of what I knew about the world. I can't go in with the wagon so I just wave at the owner. I notice he has put a silver bell on the glass door. On the corner of Fifth and Main is the most popular of the three bars on Main Street, The Lumberjack. There is a large neon sign outside of Paul Bunyan and Babe, his big blue ox. Being early, there are only a few patrons in the bar. One man, who works with my father, nods at me as he pushes through the doors. Across the street, on the other corner, is Gerlach's Drug Store. Mr. Gerlach, in his starched pharmacist's smock, stands sternly in the doorway. He does not approve of his rowdy neighbors at The Lumberjack. A high-school girl, who runs the drugstore fountain on Saturdays, waves at me. She lives near us and is famous for her cherry cokes.

One more block brings me past the bakery where I sometimes work cleaning up in the evening, while the baker spends a long dinner hour at The Lumberjack. A woman I work with is wrapping bread in the window and smiles as I walk by. She is always teasing me about girlfriends but means nothing by it. Now I am at Mr. Ohlson's grocery store. The clerks know me there. I use

my wagon to bring extra lettuce from our garden to sell there in
the summer. The butcher selects a nice bird, wraps it, and places
it in my wagon while I look around at all the people shopping.
I see several kids from my class carrying their mother's baskets.
I turn toward home on a route that takes me past the town's
largest church.

The United Methodist Church is the place where the glory of
the Lord truly shines in our town. In appearance it is certainly
a mighty fortress. There is a great square brick tower in front
with faded stained-glass windows on either side. On this day
there is more activity than usual. The local plywood mill has
given sheets of plywood to a men's committee who have cut out
and painted nativity figures. They have followed patterns from
Popular Mechanics Magazine and are setting up the figures on the
church lawn. A shepherd-boy figure near the sidewalk is taller
than me. I can hear the organist practicing inside as members
of the adult choir begin to file in for a rehearsal. The people
who attend this church are the religious core of our town. Being
from a Catholic family, and meeting for Mass in a room above
the bakery when the priest is in town, I am not officially part of
this community. But today there are lots of glad tidings directed
at me — and the turkey.

That's it. Oh, I got home with the turkey. It was a morning when nothing really happened, yet it provided a sense of
community that I have seldom felt since. I did not know that
everyone's world would change because of the war. It was not
just the horrible casualties and the gold star flags in the windows. After the tears and glory of the war, we were to become a
very prosperous nation, which was nice, but we lost some connection with each other in the process as we moved on with
the business of getting ahead. That 1941 walk in Springfield,
Oregon, becomes more present to me with each passing year.

10

RAIN

In Northern California the summers are very dry. Then there is the wonder of one late autumn day when a first gentle rain transforms the parched earth. On that day there is a balmy aroma of refreshed land — a kind of thanksgiving incense. I long to be at home on that day.

Winter rain is not always welcome. Fierce storms can bring torrential downpours. Slogging through mud and fighting erosion does not produce cherished memories for the farmer. Fighting heavy rain is futile, and Buddhist monks who live in lands with a definite rainy season have learned to use the time for a long annual retreat.

I feel a bit like the monks when I come into the city; rain falls heavily on the streets, yet I don't have to maintain the drains. For me, rain in a city is like a looping haiku poem in which familiar things are transformed. The dust of past days is washed away. Shoes may be soggy, but they are clean. The wetness creates a community of people with clean, wet shoes.

Riding with me on the T, Boston's subway system, one early December morning, college students had their heads in different books, but the wetness of their hair and clothes revealed a commonness between them. It was the same with the younger kids dripping in the aisle and the old man trying to maneuver his umbrella through the door. On some days, it is an easy jump from being soaked together in the subway car to recognizing the divine spark in each of us. Coming up to street level, I saw, next

to the exit, a pine tree with a drop of rain on every needle. Sidewalks became mirrors where all the city's lights were reflected. Everything and everyone glistened. I was in a world of shining people.

When we try to maintain planned schedules or become obsessive about destinations and tasks, rain magnifies the absurdity of our efforts. Hopefully, at such moments a kid in rubber boots will come along, splashing from puddle to puddle, often beneath disapproving adult eyes, who helps us understand the importance of being in the rain. We can travel back to the 1950s and once again look up at Gene Kelly on the screen dancing and "Singing in the rain. /Just singing in the rain. / What a glorious feeling. / I'm happy again!" Pretty corny, but it still can hit the spot.

There are many rain haiku poems. The Japanese poet Buson (1715–1753) created an image of a child's cloth ball on the roof being soaked in the rain. For me, the whole manufactured world is in that ball decomposing in the rain. Perhaps the dreams of childhood are also fading up there. The Spanish mystic Teresa of Avila (1515–1582) wrote of watering the garden of spiritual growth. Some days we must laboriously haul water from the river; at other times we may be able to use a well and an irrigation system. However, on some days it simply rains! Jack Kerouac (1922–1969) came to the same place in a rain haiku. He wrote of a bird bath filling up by itself. Now there is an image — Gene Kelly, Buson, Jack Kerouac, and Saint Teresa all dancing and singing together in the rain!

When it is raining very hard, sitting in the shelter of a coffee shop watching the rain is a pretty good non-activity. There is an awareness of the storm and an appreciation for not being in it. Perhaps this is what all those poets and those monks on the rain retreats are getting at. Sometimes it is good to stop, to discard those not-so-important-all-so-important agendas. Can sipping espresso in a coffee shop be compared to writing a haiku poem or meditating at a monastic retreat? I think so. The important thing is to acknowledge the rain and to reexamine our priorities. It does not matter too much how that is accomplished. Issa (1763–1826), one of my favorite haiku poets, was once riding along on his horse, protected by clothing, comforted by his supplies, thinking of poems to come, when he was caught in a downpour and understood who he was. He wrote:

> A sudden shower, equals
> being naked
> on a naked horse.

Rain breaks into our consciousness and suspends ordinary activities. In whatever way we can mount Issa's naked horse, we should go for it.

What goes on in the minds of all those monks on rain retreats? They are probably not thinking about how to fix the kitchen stove or who will be the next abbot. I don't know what really matters to them, but whatever it is, that is what they focus on. What does really matter to each of us? I knew nothing of Buddhist monks when, half a century ago, I was a young attorney in Oregon, a land with a very long rainy season. However, I have strong memories of driving home from the office after a first winter rain. It was as if a curtain of mist and drizzle had fallen on the stage of my professional life, providing an intermission in which to focus on what mattered most in my life: family, children, friends, peace.

It is said that the monks on rain retreats take very special care not to step on any sprout coming up at this time. They are probably equally protective of new life emerging in each of them as well. It is a good idea for all of us.

I wonder if the monks, on some dry autumn day, pray for rain. I do.

11

CHANUKAH STORIES

A T A POINT in the winter darkness each year, lights are lit to commemorate an ancient miracle. In 165 BCE, a Jewish army drove out an oppressor and reclaimed the Temple in Jerusalem. They cleaned it and removed all foreign symbols. When the time came to light the perpetual flame, as part of the rededication to divine worship, they found only enough oil to last one day. With faith, they lit the lamp anyway, and it burned for eight days — until new oil became available. In modern times, tiny candles on menorahs flicker in windows and giant gas flames shoot up from eight pipes in the city square each winter reminding us to rededicate the sacred space within each of us.

Many Jewish families gather each evening during Chanukah to light a candle, share traditional foods, and play games. All of this is a rich experience, but what attracts me the most to Chanukah are the stories. Certainly holiday stories abound at this time of year — in books, on the television, on the screen, and on the stage. Nonetheless, the Chanukah stories stand out. They portray the history of a family, a culture, a people. It is an ongoing story and one filled with hope and the promise of light in the darkness.

Most Chanukah stories celebrate our misfortunes as well as our good fortune. There is, to me, something very sad about the perfect Christmas family so often portrayed on television. When I was young, advertisements encouraged us to look through the window into the living room of a famous cowboy star and his family. No disaster ever struck there. The people were beautifully dressed — all in red. The food on the table was elegant. The tree had not a single ornament out of place. The blazing log in the fireplace was perfectly positioned. My family did not even have a fireplace!

Looking through the windows into Chanukah stories, we see: two blind children in a poor house, a dying child, the home of a struggling and oppressed family in Poland, parents coping with cold and hunger in harsh times, children surviving the Nazis in the Warsaw Ghetto, Auschwitz, a parakeet on a freezing window ledge in Brooklyn who proved to be a matchmaker with a taste for potato pancakes. No Chanukah story has ever left me feeling that my winter celebrations were not going to measure up. It has been just the opposite. They teach me to appreciate finding a little light in the murky labyrinth of my own life. And that is good enough to encourage me to keep going. Just like the original event of reclaiming the Temple and keeping the light burning, Chanukah stories focus on the ongoing process of personal rededication to whatever a person holds to be sacred.

As Jewish families and their friends celebrate Chanukah, it is a good time for us all to remember our individual, family, and planetary stories. The process, for me, begins with discarding the commercial and romantic fantasies into which I could never fit. I am never going to have a holiday dinner like a super chef on television. The children around me will never hang on my every word about the "true" meaning of Christmas. I will never live in a scene from a Christmas card. All that should be discarded. The liberation of my spirit must come within the life I am actually living.

From Chanukah stories, I have come to understand that on winter days it is sometimes good to suspend disbelief and keep an eye open for the prophet Elijah, a ninth-century BCE prophet of major proportions. He did not die, but was taken up to heaven in a fiery chariot. In time he became a sort of Jewish guardian angel who appeared when needed. He was also a reminder of the coming of the Messiah to oppressed people. In the shtetls, the villages, of Eastern and Central Europe, Elijah was often portrayed as a humble wayfarer. At the spring Passover supper, the door is opened to let him in. In many Chanukah stories Elijah finds his own way in, adding just that little bit of miracle to make sad faces turn happy. While the rest of us try to keep our eyes on the central action, Elijah looks around the margins of life to give a nudge here and there to help things come out right.

There are little rededication stories in each of us that are worth remembering and telling. For years I have wondered what a Chanukah story that I wrote would look like. I'm not Jewish and I am not a fiction writer, so what's the point? There is something very deep and universal in these stories, and I wanted to discover more about what it was by writing one. As I aged I became more fascinated by old men, and I started tucking away bits of their stories until I had a bagful. One winter day I emptied out the pieces, and what resulted was a very short story about a forgotten old man. He was not Jewish, but I hope his story resembles a Chanukah tale. Here it is.

Trevor's Letter

My friend Trevor was a deeply religious man who loathed the celebration of Christmas. "It has become a carnival," he would grouse. "It could be a healing time, but a carnival is a way of denying that you have anything to heal!" Strong stuff from a once renowned scholar on world religions. His whole life had been dedicated to encouraging people to satisfy their deep

spiritual longings. He now watched with disgust the popular arts-of-living gurus focusing on skills that, he felt, resulted in shallow and often meaningless lives. The Christmas season was the worst time of the year for him.

After his wife's death, Trevor resigned from the university and withdrew to a small cottage in Vermont. He gradually became quite sad and depressed. He had no phone or television and kept to himself. For years, his only contact with a few old friends came down to a year-end letter. The last one was sent a few months before he died.

It has rained most of December. I did not mind. Perhaps it matched my mood, which, as you well know, is none too bright at this time of year. But it will surprise you to learn that I did have a Christmas visitor. She was with me for an hour in late December.

I had been reading at the kitchen table and looked out the window to discover a child sitting on the bench in my little backyard garden. She looked to be about eight and was a stranger to me, but then I don't know most of my neighbors. I saw no reason to run her off. She seemed quite intent on something. I went back to reading, confident that she would tire of her game and move away.

Some time later I looked out and found the child still there. She seemed fascinated by something near the ground. My curiosity grew, and I stood up to see what held her attention. There, among the dried flower stalks, was a bird scratching around in the damp earth. It was one of those dull, ordinary-looking creatures that never excite you enough to look them up in a bird book. But there was a familiarity about it. His, or her, ancestors had probably been on the margin of my life since early childhood.

Something moved me to want to share the girl's moment. I opened the backdoor, considering how I could reassure her and not frighten the bird away. But it was the child who looked up and smiled at me. She quietly moved over on the bench. I took this as an invitation and joined her.

Nothing really happened after that. We sat there watching the bird. Other birds came. As they moved around the deserted garden, I felt a vigor that surprised me. This child and these birds were finding nourishment in what I thought, if I ever thought about it at all, was a decaying landscape. It seemed perfectly natural to be sitting there with a child I had never met watching birds explore the garden I had forgotten. In truth, it was a perfectly natural thing to do! It was very peaceful.

In time the birds all flew away. The child followed the last one out of the yard. She stopped at the garden gate, turned, and gave me another smile. I realized that we had not said a word. I thought it best, for the moment, to let it be that way.

Reading Trevor's letter, I remembered a phrase: "The prophet Elijah walks among us." He probably does — sometimes as an eight-year-old girl in our own backyard.

12

RISK

On damp, wintry days children seem to continually pour in and out of doorways, schools, parks, malls, movies, cars. Squads of brightly clad short people are happily and confidently occupying the same wet streets as we, slightly apprehensive, umbrella carriers. On a very cold morning, old people and young ones approach the streets very differently. My eyes are focused on the sidewalk looking for ice as I proceed slowly in perpetual fear of a fall with all the serious consequences that might entail. Around me kids romp, radiant when discovering a patch of ice and the opportunity to move fast and make this journey an exciting one. These children lavishly use the vitality that I, in my mid-seventies, must ration out. Attracted to uncertainty, they take risks to explore what is unknown, confident that if they fall they can stand up again. My energy goes into doing whatever it takes to avoid falling. I think I have something to learn from these young adventurers.

Our winter festivals are sometimes said to be all about children. That is true if we include the child we once were. Thirty years ago, Robert Duncan sent me a copy of a poem he had written. It ends:

> The boy I was
> calls out to me
> here the man where I am — Look!
> I've been where you
> most fear to be.[2]

Since that day when Robert's poem arrived, and I posted it in my study, I have been aware of the gap widening between the boy that I was and the old man that I am. Which is why I think it is important to find some remaining common ground with the children who make up the future of my world. The spiritual symbols of winter, be it the Christ Child or the enlightened Buddha, can be better understood by jumping into a mud puddle than by meditating at a sober crèche or shrine.

For me, there is a great danger of becoming numb during this season. I can easily become passive and let the commercial, religious, or entertainment world take over my life. Even kindly school teachers attempt to define my relations to my children as holidays approach. There is the school play. Three orchestra rehearsals and two performances must be fitted in somehow. The push for term papers and tests fill what space remains. Then, at the last moment, comes the call to provide transportation for a "fun" event "because it is Christmas and the children have been working so hard." All this blows toward us when what we really want is some space and time to connect with those who mean the most to us. Instead, we too often race from event to event. Then our resentment, and our exhaustion, builds. Realistically, to stand against an avalanche of seasonal school activities would be emotional suicide, unlikely to be understood by anyone — including our children. But there are times when it is possible and important to buck the dulling tide and take some risks.

It is easy for me to let old Scrooge enter my heart. It is a kind of protection from various disappointments. Like Dickens's character, I have learned that the only remedy is to be vulnerable. Often this has to do with facing a loss. My kids are in all these school and club activities rather than taking a long walk with me along a driftwood-covered beach. Someone very significant to me has died and I am convinced that I can never again have a meaningful Christmas. Illness, infirmity, or misfortune intrude. How can I possibly celebrate?

Some days, when I get fed up with what I am missing, I preach to myself in the style of an exercise coach. "All right now. Today we are going to take a risk. Any risk!" Well, it works. I can't relate many successfully completed missions, but I can list some risks I attempted in a recent year: suggesting to the school a "Family At-Home Friday" when the weekend was taken up with school holiday events; it violated state law. Calling up an old friend from whom I had been estranged; he was put off. Taking a stressed-out teenager up on a hill to watch the stars; it started to rain. Sneaking into the back pew of a large church for a shot of sacred nourishment; the priest was attacking people who cremated their relatives as being insensitive and godless cheapskates. You get the picture. But success doesn't matter. The point is that I dropped my emotional defenses and let myself be vulnerable. And sometimes there actually were special rewards. My teenage son thought the star trip was hilarious, and for months he asked what else I had planned for "quality time." One out of four attempts isn't bad, and someplace along the line I managed to lose Mr. Scrooge.

Risk is a part of the winter season. Animals starve and freeze to death. So did our ancestors. Many ancient symbols arise from the fact that there is a physical and emotional danger inherent to the season. Few understood this as well as Mary, the mother of Jesus. The stories differ, but the picture presented by Luke's gospel is of a teenaged, unmarried, young woman being asked by an angel to give birth to Jesus in a manner sure to threaten her reputation, her future happiness, perhaps her life. Every step of the way there is trouble — traveling when very pregnant, homeless when she gives birth. It is no wonder that oppressed people identify with her and find special significance in her prayer-song: "God has pulled down princes from their thrones and exalted the lowly. The hungry he has filled with good things and the rich sent empty away" (Luke 2:52–53).

Not many of us can match Mary's leap of faith, but we can accept that "Take-a-December-Risk-Day" is good for our own well-being and often for the happiness of those around us. And, in some way, it helps advance the story that begins with a young woman giving birth to great hope under very difficult conditions.

There is, for me, a revitalized sense of what it means to be alive when I have taken a few steps toward where I "most fear to be."

13

SANTA LUCIA

DARKNESS CAN BE depressing, even frightening. Under the older Julian calendar, December 13 was the shortest and darkest day of the year. For those living near the Arctic Circle, there is almost no daylight on that day and all kinds of unpleasant fantasies may abound. Which explains why a person in Sweden would be relieved to start the day by having a young girl with long golden hair, dressed in white with a wreath of seven candles on her head, pop into the bedroom to serve rolls and coffee. That's a sure way to dispel the shadows of nature and of mind!

The Scandinavian tradition of celebrations named for Santa Lucia is at least a thousand years old. Why? Recently a group of scientists "discovered" that winter darkness can cause seasonal affective disorder (SAD), resulting in loss of interest in life, feelings of worthlessness, a sense of guilt, an inability to concentrate or make decisions, even thoughts of death. What is one suggested cure? Bright Light Therapy in which the patient begins the day with thirty minutes of light from a special lamp that has roughly the equivalent intensity of ten thousand candles. For centuries, people of northern Europe have found that seven candles on a girl's head is pretty good therapy as well.

People of Scandinavian descent have a special fondness for Santa Lucia (283?–304?), who lived all her short life on Sicily. "Lucia" is derived from *lux,* a Latin word for "light." When Lucia was born, the new emperor Diocletian was trying to firm up a crumbling empire. The weird cult called Christians troubled his sense of social orderliness, so he banned them. Church legend goes that Lucia was raised in the Christian faith by her widowed mother. At some point a suitor came into the picture, interested in both the young Lucia and her sizable dowry. Lucia rejected him for she had made a vow to give her life to God. In revenge, he denounced her to the civil authorities for bringing food to outlawed Christians hiding in caves. (How could she see where she was going in a dark cave while carrying baskets of food? That's right, she put a wreath of candles on her head.) The judge sentenced Lucia to a brothel. When the soldiers came to drag her away they could not move her. The frustrated magistrate then condemned her to be burned. But the fire would not light. Lucia was finally killed by a sword through her throat. The question is: what does this saint from Catholic Sicily have to do with Protestant Sweden? There are many suggested explanations but I think it is simply that December 13 was her feast day and, long before the Reformation, King Canute had established the thirteenth as the beginning of his own month-long bright light therapy in the lands we now know as Sweden, Denmark, Norway, Iceland, and Finland.

Friends of mine remember all the children assembling before dawn on Santa Lucia Day. Each child was dressed in white, and they carried candles. The brothers, Star-Boys, had pointed caps. The girls were in long white dresses tied with red sashes. The oldest daughter wore the wreath of candles and carried a tray of coffee, sun-colored saffron buns, and ginger cookies. At first light they knocked on bedroom doors and entered each room singing a traditional song that promises the return of the light, with such lines as: "The darkness will soon take flight from the valleys of the earth." After breakfast the celebration went out to the streets, schools, offices, churches, and with special attention to the hospitals and facilities for seniors.

We all have dark hours, days, years. What better medicine than slightly impertinent white-clad children serving up coffee, rolls, and hope. Sometimes my own Lucia celebration consists of teenagers producing a breakfast with some candles stuck around it at precarious angles. There are no white robes. Jeans and T-shirts, with too much skin showing in between, is the normal dress of the day for my daughter. But that is good enough. Whatever the setting, the important message is always there — hope. Somehow the darkness of the moment recedes.

When I am on my own, I have sometimes found this a good day for random hospitality. A circle of neighbors, friends, family, colleagues, and even fellow strangers in a foreign place can be a healthy environment in which to recall that we each carry within us a promise of spring and the bloom of new life. A bit of coffee and a few rolls can increase our trust that, whatever the darkness, light will return. Nothing helps me in that process more than seeing a light in the eyes of someone facing far more troubles than myself.

In time the candles burn out, the coffee and rolls are gone, and the dark night comes again. Do the fears have to return as well? Not if we are well protected. A reflection on this day should not end without a mention of the tomte, a solitary gnome living on each Scandinavian homestead. This fellow is the guardian of little things. He has been on this specific spot of earth, where the home or farm now stands, long before the oldest member of the household was born, watching over the animals and the children while they are asleep. On his nightly rounds, he checks the locks and looks to the safety of the fires. Most of all, the tomte listens to the echoes of time long gone by and the small voices of the coming years. He hears the sounds of the stars and the earth and is a bridge between the cosmos and the sleeping household. The tomte is wise in his simplicity. He knows that each man, woman, and child, no matter what their troubles, is part of a long and beautiful story.

14

FIRST AND LAST

A WELL-KNOWN COMPOSITION was on the program of a major symphony orchestra, one the orchestra had performed many times. An interviewer asked the conductor how he could find a fresh approach to such a familiar work. "I always think," he said, "that for a few in the audience, this will be the first time they hear it. And for a few others, this will be the last time. This means we have a very serious obligation to do it well." I think he set a good example for how we should approach many things in life, including the festivals of winter, no matter how many times we have experienced them.

The Christmas when my mother died was also my son David's first Christmas. The poignant experience of someone dying just when someone else is coming to awareness does not often occur in the same house. However, such events are going on all the time in each of our communities. As with the orchestra, these first and last times put an obligation on us to take care as we journey through this season. Perhaps it helps to remember a child's first December, how very special we wanted that time to be. What we were looking to share, but didn't always know how, were concrete examples of the best values in human existence. That is not something to be bought in a store.

What do we want our children to experience? Excitement? Hope? The adventure of living together peacefully with compassion for each other? Gentleness? Forgiveness? Love? We will never nail it down completely, but we had better have our general direction fairly clear if we are to compete with electronic games promising the violent destruction of alien civilizations.

Practically, we often have to narrow our focus down to those around us. Doing something of benefit for the general community, even though inspired by a recognition of the sacred core in all people, is nonetheless challenging for anyone who watches with alarm as the calendar fills up with one special event after another at this crowded time of the year. A good alternative to a December community-service project can be found in Zen monasteries. *Inji-gyo* is a practice often translated as "secret good deeds." A monastic man or woman does surprising little things to make others sense they are living in a community of concern. The tear in a robe is mended. Bathrooms are cleaned. Clothes hung out to dry are rescued from a sudden downpour. Favorite foods show up beside a bed in the morning.

In our world it is easy to feel alone, and it is sometimes worse at this time of year. The fact is, as the bumper stickers announce, to "Practice Random Kindness and Senseless Acts of Beauty" does help. An elderly neighbor who has trouble walking will be amazed that her morning paper is next to the door and not in the driveway. A man suddenly alone and with no gift for cooking will feel his isolation fade as an only-slightly-recognized pair of children show up on his doorstep with dinner.

The process of doing secret good deeds begins with looking outside ourselves to see what is happening to others nearby. That awareness is enriching in itself. I can remember a very young child asking whether we thought an invalided neighbor would like a ride to the library. I had no idea whether Mrs. Krasner had ever been to the library, but it did start us all thinking about what she might need.

There are times when I have trouble relating to people very close to me. Sad to say, illness or aging can turn relations sour.

The years when an elderly parent is facing the frustrations of having to rely on others can be difficult. It is new ground for everyone, and regrettable mistakes will be made. The teenage years of flopping around for a direction and an identity can also be trying on everyone in a family. Being an older parent, I know tension is sometimes just a matter of my not having the energy to keep up with an adolescent for whom everything is "now!" There are times when my emotional timing will be off enough to result in a breach in my relationship with a child I love. My experience is not unique. We don't have to be helplessly trapped in those difficult times. We have a lot of history with those we love, which can help to give us a more authentic sense of our relationships.

When my emotions do not mesh with those of my children, I need to transcend that tightness. I think back to the excitement of preparing for that child's entry into life. What a wonderful time it was. There are so many poignant memories of the years when we participated together in the wonder and adventure of this season. I also can cast ahead and think of the years to come and how important those times will be to me — and to them.

The death of a parent is a spiritual milestone in everyone's path. When my mother was close to death, it was easy to recall our many Christmases together. Sitting by her bed, I remembered the depression years when money was scarce and she brought the "Christmas Spirit" into our home pretty much exclusively through her own personality. Once, when I was an adult facing some difficult decisions, she simply came down the stairs one December midnight and silently joined me in looking at the lighted tree. It was a very important moment.

December has not always been a good month for me. I have faced the death of someone I loved on a number of occasions. It was one of those dear friends, only days before his death from AIDS, who said to me, "I am not going to let this disease define my Christmas." And he didn't. I vividly recall his stories of a New England childhood. The houses, the snow, the people waving from their porches, and the sense of community were, I believe, much more real to him than the dozens of pill bottles on the dresser of his West Hollywood bedroom. Thinking of my friend, I recalled that my father's last words to my mother, near midnight on Christmas Eve, were "Merry Christmas." Then he smiled and died. I think he had escaped time and was living in the saga of their thirty-four Christmas-times together, including the joys and hopes of youth as well as later challenges, which their deep affection for Christmas always seemed to alleviate. I believe he collected all their Decembers into their final moments together. I hope my mother had the same awareness and comfort when she died twenty-three years later, also on Christmas Eve.

Some months before she died my mother, with the aid of a powerful magnifying glass, helped sew and stuff some cloth ornaments for our tree. There was one of a young girl with a dog. It reminded her of a dog she had loved as a teenager. When the ornament was finished, she carefully explained to a wide-eyed David that this was for his first Christmas tree. The ornament was in its proper place on the tree when she died. David, now in his early twenties, has seen that it has been on our tree every year since.

15

THE TREE

T HE DAY OUR TREE goes up, I think of Charles Dickens. Not his Christmas stories, but the first line of *A Tale of Two Cities:* "It was the best of times, it was the worst of times." In my family, the worst comes first.

Around our house there are now acres of peaceful olive trees, but when the children were young we had a plantation of Christmas trees. We shipped hundreds of perfectly shaped trees around the country. When it came to our own tree, the children did not want one from the fields, preferring a "natural tree" from the surrounding woods. But it had to look at least as good as the trees we were raising for sale. Finding a perfect "natural tree" is quite a problem, and as the children have grown they have become ever more rigid in their individual definitions of "perfect."

When our century-old farmhouse had to be replaced, arguments over where the Christmas tree would stand in the new house had to be resolved before the architect could design the main floor. The tree became the keystone of the design. There is even a special electric plug so that if the power fails, as it often does out in the country, the tree lights will be connected to the backup generator that runs the farm equipment. The tree had always touched the ceiling in the old house. To the children, the fact that the new house has a fourteen-foot ceiling simply means that each year we need to find a fourteen-foot, natural, perfect tree. This Herculean task often seems to occur in the

early hours of a rainy day. It lasts all morning, and is guaranteed to bring out the worst in everyone.

Bringing in the tree is not a sentimental enterprise. A tree that large must be cut by chainsaw. Getting it in from the woods involves at least six people and probably a cart or tractor. There is much yelling about stepping on prize branches and the unequal distribution of the weight. Once at the house it becomes annually obvious that a fourteen-foot tree is going to be about seven feet wide at one point. Fitting it through a three-foot door is not easy. We always do it somehow and, with great physical effort, manage to get it upright and into a stand holding five gallons of water. The trunk is then anchored to hooks that are firmly attached to the house's support beams.

I am aware that people who lead more normal lives buy a six-foot tree at the corner lot and happily cart it home humming a carol or two. My purpose here is to definitively establish that I am not a romantic when it comes to the logistics of bringing trees into homes. There is a legend that Martin Luther (1483 – 1546) took a Christmas Eve walk and so admired the stars shining through a fir tree that he brought a tree home and put candles on it for his children. It is a sweet tale but apocryphal. Our Christmas trees have a very pagan origin. Centuries before Christianity came to Northern Europe, the indoor tree was part of the fear and hope of the Yule season at the time of the winter solstice. Gifts were hung in its branches to placate the gods and shining objects were added to remind the household that spring would return. I also realize that a Christmas tree can be a painful symbol to many non-Christians who have tried hard to remain true to their religious heritage in a sometimes hostile environment. The Jewish parent in an interfaith family may put up a tree "for the children's sake," but often with a sense of denial and betrayal to his or her ancestors. I understand all these things. Yet I really love the trees that have loomed over our annual festivities.

Once our tree stands in its five gallons of water and is anchored to the supports in the walls, we look on it with an awed respect once reserved for royalty. For the next month this tree is the head of our household. Brought in as a guest, it has immediately become the host.

Where there is a Christmas tree, it is the totem of that household. Decorator trees are for magazines and department stores. In the living room, we need a lot of imperfect little things on the branches that tell the story of the people in the home. The remembering starts with unwrapping, slowly, the ornaments from past years. These little things are true treasures, each a piece of the epic of the household. There is often a special ancient item or two. We have an old Santa that my parents hung on my first tree and a set of stuffed cloth ornaments made for our oldest child's first tree. A variety of slightly misshapen contributions usually come from early school arts and crafts projects and are now treasured relics. Some ornaments were bought with a particular person in mind and are tender and beautiful. Others come from trips or adventures. Gentle jokes and solemn religious symbols co-exist together harmoniously. And so it goes. In our home the anxiety and frustrations of the morning tree expedition slowly give way to warm and happy feelings.

The young people in my life assume we are all immortal. I don't. The year's toll of health problems and the challenges of being in my mid-seventies help me appreciate that my future Christmases are numbered. Therefore, it is really important to me to be aware of each ornament and each person in the room, so I contrive to be a bottleneck in the decorating process in order to slow it down. Stubbornly I insist on putting hangers properly on each ornament before it can go on the tree. And I do it slowly. As the children get older they wonder what is so difficult about putting a wire hanger on an ornament, but they are generally tolerant.

There are usually grand moments in the process of decorating a tree. For us, one is putting a large homemade star on the very top. Remember, this is fourteen feet off the floor and the child insisting on going up the ladder has sometimes been of tender years. Watching as he or she leans from the tall ladder toward the treetop, I have no doubt that we are violating numerous child-endangerment statutes. But each kid has always managed to put the star on splendidly before a silent and worried audience who shout appreciatively as the deed is done.

Each home has a different drama, but the moment always comes when the decorating is finished and the lights go on to euphoric sighs. Now the cider can be passed around and songs sung. Yes, if someone wants to sleep under the tree, it can be arranged. And, of course, this is truly the most beautiful tree ever. It really is because somehow it contains our ever-maturing love and respect for one another.

At our home, it is a very tired crew that eats supper around the newly decorated tree. I make sure it falls to me to turn off the lights on that first night. It is usually pretty late, and there may be a child or two in sleeping bags who must doze off first. I don't mind. The memories of this moment in past years come rushing in. The only light is from the tree, reflected on the tranquil ornaments and the softly moving silver tinsel. Here really stands a totem telling our family's story. I try to read it anew. Finding the old Santa, I make sure he has a prominent place, and in doing so I touch something of my own beginning.

Finally it is time for the day to end. Just before turning off the lights, I face the tree. In that deep and still space, I am aware of something from this wondrous sight telling me, "I am back."

16

SHADOWS

THERE ARE GOING TO BE difficult winter days. For one thing, nature is hard and living things die in this season. Neighborhood birds that brought us so many songs in summer are fighting for their lives in the storms and cold. Not many humans have to worry about that unless we are among those wandering homeless in our affluent streets. What many of us do suffer at some time is the painful attempt to emotionally survive on the margins of the jubilant Christmas crowds.

So many personal realities do not fit into the myth of holiday cheer. Look in any neighborhood, and you will find someone who is recently unemployed and worried about providing for those who look up to him or her. Thoughts of gifts must give way to concerns over the most basic of family needs. In some family down the street, a child who once, years ago, stared in awe at a Christmas tree is now a teenager wandering alone in some place unknown to her parents. This time of year there are many reasons for empty places at the table. Keep walking down the street. Old leaders who make wars may be pictured in the media as they celebrate the season, but the young people fighting in those horrid conflicts are not celebrating, nor are those they left at home. And everywhere in every neighborhood are people coping with the universal challenges of aging and illness. Death may be near in some homes, or already have taken someone who was so essential to our experience of this season that we cannot conceive of ever entering into it again. And who can predict when the fogs of anxiety and depression, so common to our age, will settle upon us? Behind many doors neighbors are struggling with issues simply coming from being a woman or a man in these challenging times. It has always been this way.

And let us never forget poor Joseph. He was engaged to the young Mary. A Jewish betrothal in his day was a powerful thing, and his brought joy to this village carpenter. Then, as Matthew's gospel puts it, "... before they came to live together she was found to be with child." Whoa! All dreams and hearts are broken. But Joseph loves Mary and takes her to his home, undoubtedly causing much clucking in the village. No time to worry about that. As soon as the baby is born, some foreign soothsayers appear with gifts. In the process they manage to upset brutal and insecure old King Herod with talk about an "infant king of the Jews." An angel shows up in Joseph's dream and tells him to get out of there quick! Go to Egypt he says. Egypt! How can he provide for his family there? They will be undocumented aliens! He doesn't even speak the language. No time to think; Herod's bloody soldiers are on the way. Talk about anxiety! This is a story J. R. R. Tolkien could have written.

When we turn the pages over to Luke's gospel, we find Joseph doesn't fare any better. Luke's story has Joseph and Mary living in Nazareth when she is almost ready to deliver. This is their first child, and we can assume that Joseph has all the normal concerns of a new father. He has made a cradle and he has arranged everything. Mary's family will help. The midwife is standing by. Then, with no warning, comes the order from the Romans: "Everybody go to your ancestral hometowns and register for the census." His wife is going to have the baby at any time! Joseph might have argued with the authorities that the order surely could not apply to a woman in Mary's condition. In the good old rigid Roman tradition, he would have been told that rules are rules. So off the couple goes on a trip of about seventy-five miles. Mary is focused on the miracle of new life. Joseph would have liked to do that too, but there are basic issues to face, like where can they stay. He has had no family in Bethlehem for generations. They arrive in the town as night is coming on. Mary is beginning to have labor pains. Sure enough, there is no room for them at the one inn. This is a homeless couple in desperate circumstances. Nothing is going as he had planned for the birth. Joseph gets Mary to a stable just in time for the child to be born. It is not really helpful when a bunch of shepherds push in babbling about angels. What now? He needs food, warmth, baby clothes — a welcome wagon and a crisis counselor.

Some of Joseph's stress is reenacted today in the Posada days held among people of Mexican descent. For nine days before Christmas, the drama of looking for lodging, *posada*, is acted out. A young boy trying to guide a reluctant donkey carrying an unsteady girl has its tense moments as of old. Even though there is no room to be found for the Holy Family, the strain is alleviated on the last day when the time comes to break the piñata. Each child swinging the bat is blindfolded, but eventually the satisfying crack of the piñata resounds and small treasures come raining down. We can learn from that.

Not long ago, I was diagnosed with early prostate cancer. Because of the treatments, I was often tired as December unfolded. Tasks I had happily performed in past years became burdens. Then came the wake-up call: "Do what is important to you and forget the rest!" I threw away my Christmas script and, in my own way, broke a piñata. Because of my cancer, I had learned that it is important to avoid emotional demands we cannot meet at sensitive times. Nonetheless, it is not good to simply hide off in the shadows and wait for Christmas to go away. Even though

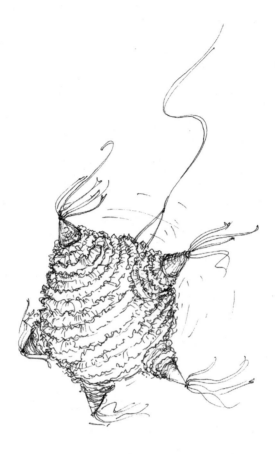

we may not always be sure of what we are doing, it is healthy to
swing our bat, hoping to crack open something that brings us
delights. There are many ways of releasing such joys. I know of
several Jewish families who have a great feast on Christmas day
at a local Asian restaurant. Spiritual groups hold special services
restricted to those who have lost someone who made Christmas
meaningful to them. One Episcopal widower I know goes to a
silent Quaker meeting the Sunday before Christmas. On Christmas day he sits with an old friend, also widowed. They have a

glass of wine before the fire. The common wisdom in all these activities is to find a temporary community and overcome the sense of alienation at this time of year. Above all, these things must be simple.

When we see people planning for the perfect Christmas, we should think of Joseph, patron saint of the imperfect Christmas. And if nothing else comes to mind, let us hang up a piñata and bang away hard.

17

THE FIRST GREAT O

THE WEEK BEFORE Christmas is a clarion call for someone with my background. The time of the great O antiphons is here! Never heard of them? What kind of a monastery did you grow up in anyway? OK, spending most of my high school years up on a hill in a Benedictine seminary was a bit weird in many ways, but the sound of an O antiphon still jazzes me. I can remember schlepping along the abbey's marble halls before Vespers humming "O Ad-on-ai," but that is the one for December 18. What am I going on about? Let's go back about 1,100 years.

Vespers is the evening prayer in the monastic tradition. It came from Jewish practices at the time of Jesus. Anglicans use the beautiful name "Evensong" for it. The Song of Mary, the Magnificat, which has inspired many composers through the centuries, is a high point in Vespers. It is a rouser of a song, opening with: "My soul proclaims the greatness of the Lord" and containing lines like "God has pulled down princes from their thrones and exalted the lowly." Each time the Magnificat is sung in the monastic choir, an antiphon, a short poignant verse, comes before and sets the mood. To me there are no antiphons like the great Os! For about three weeks monks have been singing sweet little pious or sentimental Advent antiphons, and suddenly on December 17 there is a sea change, and the choir bursts out with what we all really lack spiritually and want deeply from Christmas. It is a moment of honest hunger and serious supplication.

In 1853 two English clergymen, Thomas Helmore and John Mason Neale, put together an adaptation of the O antiphons with some music that may have been twelfth-century plain chant, and the result was the popular hymn "O Come, O Come, Emmanuel." It sounds good, especially with an organ, but I prefer one O antiphon a day sung in a more hardy and rustic mode. The antiphons are known by the first words of each one: "O Sapientia" (Wisdom), "O Adonai" (Lord), "O Radix Jesse" (Root of Jesse), "O Clavis David" (Key of David), "O Oriens" (Dawn), "O Rex" (King), "O Emmanuel" (God with us). In each antiphon there is a "Come and ... " followed by supplications, such as "teach us the way," "be with us," "enlighten us," or "free the imprisoned." Just to make it more interesting, in medieval times the official who intoned the first words of an O antiphon had to provide a treat for the whole monastery after Vespers. That alone would get the attention of a bunch of fasting monks.

A slightly amused friend, not used to seeing me excited by church music, asked what was so special about the O antiphons for me. The answer has something to do with going deep into tradition, way beyond dogmas and institutions. Back so far that common roots are found — authentic mantras that can give vitality to the week before Christmas. The "O" is a drum beat asking me to stop protecting myself emotionally and to become aware of my inner needs. How can this work today? Most of us are not surrounded by quiet cloisters and plain chant, but by freeways and honking horns. What good is it to obsess about old, largely unknown, church songs? Let's go at it another way. In this final week before Christmas, most of us are living out agendas that are thrust upon us. These include the expectations of family and friends, society's "Ho-ho-ho" mentality, our own personal traditions, and events we've been asked to organize or attend. In spite of these things-to-do, or perhaps because

of them, there is also in each of us the desire to experience something that only comes when we have pushed all the seasonal obligations out of the way.

Forget monasteries for a moment. The fundamental assumption of the Christmas story, as well as of Ramadan, Bodhi Day, or Chanukah, is that the divine and the human can touch. Don't be distracted by the church, the brocaded vestments, gold chalices, clouds of incense, and sometimes much flawed leadership. Simple things matter. Moses found holy ground at the burning bush. Jesus was born in a barn. The Quran was revealed in a cave. Siddhartha sat under a tree. The Hopi Butterfly Maiden is near a mound of corn deep in the earth. The monk finds a creator God in the rain dripping from the eaves outside his little room. Whatever we are prepared to recognize as sacred is going on now as much as it was in the dim past. The touching of heaven and earth at the birth of Jesus continues in the moment between two old friends in a coffee shop or in a family singing songs around a fireplace. Those of us raised in a Christian culture must reject the concept that Christmas is only memorializing what happened two thousand years ago. We have the opportunity to experience the same wonder in the moment we are living now.

Admittedly, I am a bit caught up in the O antiphons. What I get from them this week doesn't have much to do with the words. I hear them as a call to act as if life were truly blessed, to really be open to the sacredness reflected in my family and friends, in my community, in my world — in me. Quakers have long worked at putting this concept into practical terms. They call on us to respect in every human being, including ourselves, and in the world around us, the unfolding creative power of God. No matter what vocabulary we use, we help ourselves and each other when we open ourselves to the divine spark, the light, in the darkness that often surrounds us.

The small Benedictine monastery in Weston, Vermont, has a special focus on peace and reconciliation. The monks, uncomfortable with words of monarchy and power, changed the O antiphon for December 22 from "O King of the Gentiles" to "Bearer of Peace." They go on to solicit a "oneness of heart" with each other. I like that. Tranquility is one of the fruits of the sacred, and it does rest on a oneness of heart, though not necessarily of mind, among those who seek peace in Hopi kivas, in monasteries, in coffee shops, on the highways, around the hearth.

All together now: "O Ad-on-ai...."

18

THE HURDY-GURDY MAN

"IN THE BLEAK MIDWINTER," as Gustav Holst's (1874–1934) carol puts it, "frosty wind made moan." There is nothing like a gloomy day to bring out the moans — lots of moans. There are some days when we simply turn a corner and run into a question like "What is the meaning of my life?" And if we are not soon distracted, that leads to some pretty intense thoughts on our lives and the unfolding of our civilization. When we are in that mode, nothing can stop the memories of things we regret and the inevitable conclusion that our life has not been perfect. As we age, the future comes closer to the present. Frailty, mental decline, and care facilities begin to loom large in the minds of people my age. If we surrender completely to those thoughts we will be captured, and often disabled, by an emotional tidal wave. This is the time to look for a hurdy-gurdy man, or woman.

What is a hurdy-gurdy? It was originally a stringed instrument played, not with a bow, but with a wheel turned with the right hand while the left hand played the melody on a few keys. In time, some instruments were also designed to produce a few programmed tunes, and people with no musical talent could play them by simply turning the wheel. This became popular with street musicians, who were called hurdy-gurdy men. The instrument produces a loud, rather coarse sound, something like a bagpipe, and will definitely get your attention.

Outside of a brief gig with my second-grade rhythm band, I have never played an instrument or seriously studied music.

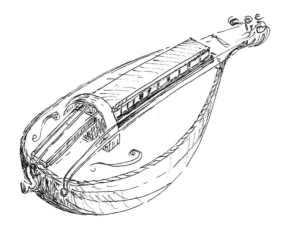

However, I approach concert halls with the reverence I once re-served for cathedrals. I am a very devout member of the audience. All the technical explanations go over my head. I only know that through music I can experience the sacred. My first encounter with a hurdy-gurdy man as a symbol of a commonplace balance to life's tempests was through a memory that the composer Gustav Mahler (1860–1911) related to the psychoanalyst Sig-mund Freud (1856–1939.) In his compositions, Mahler used great and noble concepts, but he was frustrated by the musi-cal resolution often being "spoiled," as he saw it, by something mundane. Others have seen this same phenomenon as part of his genius, but what matters here is how the composer saw it.

Mahler's father, a non-observant Jew trying to fit into a con-servative Catholic culture, dominated a gloomy household where eight children died. Mahler had a deep emotional attachment to his mother who, despite her frailty, must have been an an-chor in the changing circumstances of family life. The father was a violent man who regularly abused his wife. Mahler told Freud that in the midst of one especially vicious scene he ran from the house, consumed with horror and helplessness. As the young Mahler emerged on the street he came face-to-face with a hurdy-gurdy man loudly playing the hackneyed "Ach, du lieber Augustin." Something had to give! Perhaps at that moment Mahler comprehended that life could be absurd. No matter how real and strong an experience might be, it is not the only reality. The hurdy-gurdy man, with his cloddish song, is also real.

"Ach, du lieber Augustin" originated during the plague that devastated Vienna in 1768. The song has the reoccurring line "Everything is gone!," which must have resonated with the fleeing Mahler. The story goes that a musical performer, Max Augustin, lost all his friends, his money, and his girlfriend to the plague. He went to an inn, drowned his sorrows with wine, passed out on his way home, was assumed to be a plague victim, and was carted away by the morning corpse patrol. Augustin awoke just in time to avoid being buried. Perhaps Mahler snapped out of his trauma just in time to avoid being emotionally buried.

A couple of centuries after Max Augustin, the popular British singing artist Donovan (1946–) went with his friends the Beatles on a spiritual pilgrimage in India, where he wrote:

> Down through all eternity
> The crying of humanity.
> 'Tis then when the Hurdy-Gurdy Man
> Comes singing songs of love.[3]

When the certainty of ill health or old age comes into sharp focus, the hurdy-gurdy man can bring another essential comfort, found in a song cycle by Franz Schubert (1797–1828). In 1827 Schubert came across some poems by Wilhelm Müller and used them to compose *Winterreise* ("Winter Journey") which he completed that October. He died a year later, two months before his thirty-second birthday.

Winterreise consists of twenty-four segments on the desolate journey of a wanderer who has been deeply disappointed in love. He travels through cold and bleak places, which he once encountered in times of happiness and warmth. There is no place for him, even in the village graveyard. He never meets another person until, in the final song, he comes upon a hurdy-gurdy man.

Many, perhaps most, commentators see the hurdy-gurdy man in *Winterreise* as Death. It is true that Schubert finished the work when his physical condition was deteriorating rapidly from advanced syphilis. He had entered the terminal stage. However, there is evidence that Schubert did not know he was dying and was making important plans for future studies, compositions, and performances. What Schubert did undoubtedly realize was the typical course of this well-known disease for which there was, at that time, no cure. He had lived with the symptoms and the treatments for five years, and he knew that the pain, the inability to use his limbs, the fever, and the hospitalizations would increase. And in the end, there would be dementia. Syphilis is no longer the sexually transmitted disease we most fear, but Schubert's situation sounds painfully familiar to those of us who have watched the deterioration of young friends or family living with AIDS. Was Schubert contemplating this suffering when his wanderer ran into a hurdy-gurdy man? I side with those who think he was. Even amongst such horrible specters, relief can be found.

The song describes the hurdy-gurdy man as tottering barefoot on the ice. Like Schubert, whose work had not yet received the recognition it was to attain, the old man had no money in his small plate: "no reward to show. / No one wants to listen."[4] Only the dogs growl around him. Nonetheless, the hurdy-gurdy man does not stop playing his one song. He has "numb fingers" and yet "plays as best he can." This is the lesson I hear, for all of us in whatever our circumstance — to play as best we can.

What does Schubert do when he stands face-to-face with his own grim future? Will this be his end as a result of the disease, his creative powers reduced to repeating a few songs mechanically and mindlessly over and over again? This could be the ultimate moment of despair, but the mood lightens, or more accurately, the horizon expands and the wanderer senses the whole human condition. Peace comes with our full acceptance of being a part of that larger story.

The last verse in *Winterreise* is, for me, sublimely transcendent:

> Curious old fellow,
> shall I go with you?
> When I sing my songs,
> will you play your hurdy-gurdy too?

And off they go together, the wanderer and the hurdy-gurdy man, playing as best they can with numbed fingers.

Thus *Winterreise* ends. There is only silence. But I know Schubert is singing. And the old man cranks out the song as best he can. It is good enough, for any of us.

Franz Schubert did not descend into a long madness. He had three days of delirium and great pain. Then, shortly before he died, he was lucid and asked to be buried near Beethoven. In 1888 his grave and Beethoven's were moved and they are now beside each other in a place of honor. The more important memorial is that every day their music encourages and inspires people on their journeys though life.

The chances are that most of us will not run into many men or women playing hurdy-gurdys. But we should be aware that the hurdy-gurdy man comes in different guises: the band on the street corner, the grade-school choir, the local Nutcracker dancers, the Girl Scouts caroling at the door, the Salvation Army volunteer ringing his bell. All play as best they can, and all can broaden our horizons when we are engulfed by weighty concerns. The hurdy-gurdy man is out there. Believe it.

For many, this is a deeply religious season celebrating the birth of a divine savior who came to dwell among us. Some might ask, "Where is God in all this music stuff?" It is a good question, but I can only repeat, the hurdy-gurdy man, or woman, is out there — singing songs of love as best he or she can. I think we should do the same.

19

VINEYARD

EVERY SATURDAY NIGHT the Jewish day of rest, Shabbat, ends with a prayer that can only be recited after three stars have been sighted. The prayer blesses God, who can help us make the transition from the sacred to the secular. With that prayer, *Navdalah,* ordinary life resumes. The natural rhythm of any farmer's life makes a similar transition at this time of year, but in reverse — from the ordinary to the wondrous.

In California, where I live, anything can be found at Christmas: Santas surfing into shore or arriving in hot-air balloons, children of every ethnicity singing in the old Franciscan missions, medieval festivals in a national park, torchlight skiing in the mountains, earnest birders making the Christmas bird count. And in my county, some men and women standing tranquilly in vineyards, for no reason at all.

On my way home from town, I drive through a beautiful valley. The first peoples knew it as a treasure-house of reeds, roots, and pure water from which beautiful baskets were woven, remedies for health produced, and contact with the divine established. The European-American settlers cleared off the trees and brought cattle. Their grandchildren filled the valley with plum trees for prunes. In winter the trees were bare, twisted, and stern. But in the spring, the whole valley was vibrant with pink blossoms. The grandchildren of the prune growers cleared the land again and planted grapes. Upscale wineries replaced dingy drying sheds.

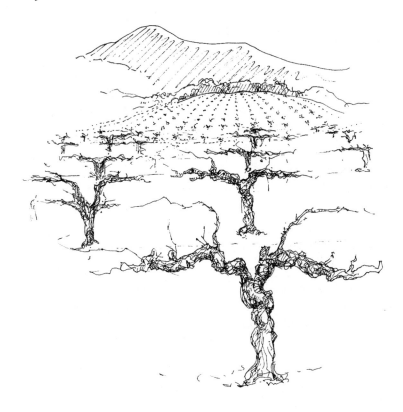

Since the wine culture took hold, the valley can be quite a circus at times. Land speculators are selling vineyards, and an aristocratic lifestyle, to wealthy buyers. Recent owners who have moved up from the corporate castles of Los Angeles impress their city friends with recently acquired rural wisdom. Grand motor coaches, limousines, and luxury cars park beside dusty Fords with Midwestern license plates. They all bring hordes of tourists, ready to be impressed by salespeople in tasting rooms who direct them to discover the subtle dried blackberry or vanilla peppercorn flavors in the zinfandel. People on wine tours come from everywhere, Australia to Alabama, and crisscross the main

road with cameras and souvenir wine glasses. They are happy.
The owners are happy. The tourist industry is ecstatic. When
harvest time arrives in early autumn, trucks and tractors replace
the fancy vehicles on the road. Life in the valley is purified by
twenty-four hour workdays and the satisfaction of the press-
ing. People born in the valley sleepily congregate with former
stockbrokers in very downscale cafes that have catered to harvest
crews for many years.

By November the grapes have long been stripped from gnarled
grey vines. Work crews, machinery, and the hectic pace of the
harvest are usually gone. The autumn rains have cut down on
visitors. In December, the only buses on the road are those
taking children to and from school. Driving through the valley
at this time of year, I often see solitary farmers walking down
the rows of vines now emptied of their grapes. They could be
owners, but more likely they are first or second generation Latino
workers.

In the fading light of a winter day there is only quiet in the
vineyards. I stop the car, step out, and try to become a part of
the still reality of the moment. A remnant of yellow, brown, and
crimson leaves hangs loosely on the vines, at the foot of the
blue hills. Across the road a brown-skinned man walks between
the rows of vines. There is a young boy with him. They stop
and do what all those who have walked this land have done. The
father remembers the frantic adventures of life in that field.
The child is awed to be in his father's world as the sun sets. I
think, like me, they are watching for the first star, open to the
movement from the ordinary to the sacred. "Grateful" is the
feeling I probably share with this man — the appreciation of
being alive and well and taking a deep breath in this beauty. For
my silent companion across the road, there may be more to it.

Where was he last year? Working to bring his family up north? If so, is it all that different from the biblical tale of the Holy Family's flight into the safety of Egypt? According to the story in Matthew's gospel, Joseph was fleeing to avoid Herod's massacring soldiers. This man across the road from me is probably also a decent protector of his family who broke a number of laws to get them here. Somehow he moved from "illegal" to reluctantly tolerated, then proved his worth in the field and became accepted. How fragile the plan must have been at times. The stakes were high and the dangers great. There must have been some frightening moments he will never share with anyone. Now, he probably has a house nearby, which would indicate that he has a responsible position. This year there is safety from poverty and fear for his family. His children will probably feel less disapproval from the white culture than he has endured. Though there may still be some discrimination, his children will become more "fully American" with all the good and bad that brings with it.

Did Joseph also walk out with Jesus, on an evening in some Egyptian field? Did he have the same feelings as the father across the road? It doesn't have to be in Egypt or in a Sonoma County vineyard. Every parent has seen the future blur while comforting a child whose dreams have been shattered, reaching for one who has taken a wrong and dangerous turn, supporting one who is fighting to overcome obstacles, or sitting helpless beside a hospital bed. As the crisis passes, "Thank God!" spontaneously springs out of us. The newborn Jesus would have needed to know nothing beyond his mother's breast. As he grew, whatever happened, he would learn to simply look into Joseph's face to see whether everything was still all right in his little world. The experiences of all parents seem to link together on such a night as this. I wish one of my children were with me. Of course, in some way, they are, but still I am aware of my solitary position. The child across the road notices me and points me out. Looking my way, the father waves. I wave back. They turn and slowly walk away hand in hand. It is darker now. Dinner is probably going on their table. As it is at my house as well. I get back into my car.

Just before I turn the key, I glance down the road. In the middle of the next vineyard a string of lights has been wrapped around a single gnarled grapevine. Above, the stars of night are now clearly visible. Is there a prayer that goes "Blessed are you, O Lord, who helps us find the sacred in a vineyard"?

There is now.

20

THE 11:48

Some important things did not come with us into the twenty-first century. One of these is the sound of trains at Christmas. I don't mean contemporary silver streaks with names like *Eurostar* or *The Bullet*. I remember big, black, powerful steam engines that were referred to by the time they arrived at a station.

I don't know why the train became so associated with Christmas in the past century. Perhaps it had something to do with families separating to settle across the continent in the nineteenth century. The first scheduled American passenger train was inaugurated in 1830 — on Christmas day. When we were in faraway places, a train could bring us home or bring home to us. After my father died, my mother would take the train from her home in Oregon to California. She arrived in a trainload of grandmothers whose families overflowed the Oakland train station. Our holidays began when she stepped off the train. The situation was reversed years before when I was an unhappy adolescent in a monastic boarding school. All during December I would dream of the train that would take me away from my disapproving tutors. At last the day would come when the hissing giant came down the track to rescue me. When I was a few years younger, an even bigger train had rescued Christmas itself.

Eight of the 11:48's fourteen wheels were more than six feet tall. Its whistle pierced the lonely night and echoed against the mountains. It came down from the dark and cold Cascade peaks into Western Oregon, its freight cars capped with snow. The first stop was the station at Springfield, the little lumber town where I was raised 65 years ago.

On the day before Christmas in 1941, when I was ten years old, the United States had been at war for seventeen days. I didn't know what that meant, but I could feel my world changing. Already flags with blue stars were appearing in some of the windows on my street, one star for each son or daughter in the armed services. My father was out with the other fathers at night, preparing a defense against unknown threats. My mother, like all the other mothers, attempted to keep things normal. But Christmas and war don't coexist easily. Silent night. Fearful night.

I suspected that Christmas, as I knew it, was really being canceled that year. Certainly the school play was canceled, and the midnight Mass. The nightly blackouts had begun. A neighborhood warden would quietly tap on your front door and whisper that a bit of light could be seen from the kitchen window, and someone would whisper back a thanks and run to adjust the thick drapes. For me, the quiet on those nights was filled with dread.

Laying in my bed on that Christmas Eve, I was sad for the loss of a magical and wonderful time. Then I heard the first deep whistle of the 11:48. For as long as I could remember, I had heard that sound as I walked into midnight Mass. Our church did not ring the bell at night for fear of disturbing the neighbors, most of whom had enough trouble understanding Catholics as it was. For me the mighty whistle of the 11:48, growing in strength and frequency as it came into the station, was the beginning of Christmas Mass. And here it was again. War could not stop it. Somewhere out there was something more powerful than tragedy. Christmas was on that train. Perhaps I even thought God was on that train, the God whose presence I have never questioned in hard times.

As I have aged, there have been a lot of hard times for me at Christmas. I think the roughest have been when a child or a parent, or someone else I deeply loved, was very ill and the question was there: "Is this our last Christmas together?" The Christmas after we parted was not easy either, as most people know from experience. I have been close to a number of friends and neighbors who also have empty places at Christmas. At this time of year, children no longer with us come most to mind: Deirdre, the sparkling little Irish dancer; Tina, who loved the songs of the season; Jennifer, who died within days of her mother; Isabel, who had an underdeveloped brain but a smile that changed many lives; Josh, who loved red; Chester, who died of his father's abuse; and children I have known here and in other countries who lived with joy and died with dignity in the AIDS pandemic. Faces. So many lovely faces.

There have also been rocky times with my own health, physical or mental, and similar concerns about those I love. A spark inside me wants to bring the special glow of Christmas into the eyes of a child. But as I grow older, and less sure of my ability to cope with life, sometimes I cannot keep up with the energy around me and, at times, much to my regret, I even dampen young spirits I could once inflame.

So it is that there is sometimes pain as I sit in silence with those I love beside the hearth, or rock with a sleeping child, just before Christmas. At those times, I am waiting for it. And it comes — the driving pistons and deep whistle of the 11:48. Oh yes, I still hear it. A train like that makes a sound that echoes for a long time. How long? I don't know, but for more than 65 years so far. On those nights when things are not so good, I am now sure that there has been something sacred about the

11:48. Those women and men I have loved and cherished — my parents, my children, and many others I miss deeply — are all on it now.

Someday perhaps I too will be on board that train. But until that time, I know that the 11:48 is there to remind me, and anyone else who wants to listen, that some things cannot be stopped — and love at Christmas is one of them.

21

A HUMANISTIC SOLSTICE

T HE ROOTS OF OUR OBSERVANCE of Christmas are strong, ancient, and often pagan. Much comes from the celebration of what the Romans termed "solstice" — the day the sun stood still. But long before the Romans, the first people in the Northern Hemisphere watched with fear as the sun sank lower in the sky each day and the life-giving sunlight diminished. Then came the moment when it seemed to stop disappearing. Calculating by our present calendar this takes place about December 21–22. In the days following, it seemed to our ancestors that the sun was slowly returning to the earth as it rose higher and remained longer in the sky. And so, by what we now label December 25, it was clearly a time to rejoice. Throughout the centuries, people hoped that, despite appearances, each winter darkness would be lifted. All over the world there are sites with stones aligned to catch the first rays of the sun on the winter solstice.

In time, public festivals evolved. Egypt celebrated the virgin-born Osiris's return to life and the renewal of fertility to the land when the Nile flooded annually. Dionysus, the Greek harvest god, was torn apart by fierce women and then reborn as a baby. In the north of Europe, where the sun actually did completely disappear for a time, the sometimes wild celebration of Yule released the season's tensions. In the century before Jesus, the Roman Saturnalia spread through the Empire. This was a frenzied celebration that lasted many days and was much loved by the people. The social order was turned upside down. Drink flowed freely. Many normal sexual restrictions evaporated. As the power of Christianity grew, there was a desire to tone down this popular annual revelry. In the fourth century, without much historical foundation, December 25 was designated as the birthday of Jesus. This date was already celebrated as the birthdays of the sun god Sol Invictus and the popular Persian god Mithras. The plan worked. There is not a lot of Roman debauchery going on these days, except at the odd office party. It is important to recognize, however, that a part of the powerful attraction of Christmas today goes back to pre-Roman times — to the earth itself.

We took a distracting detour with Victorian Christmases. These images still fill our imagination, but they come not from a sense of the sacred but from the nineteenth-century British idolization of a perfect, if mythical, domestic life. And, much to the delight of the growing merchant class, presents came on the scene in a big way. As Jo March put it in Louisa May Alcott's (1832–1888) *Little Women,* "Christmas won't be Christmas without any presents." God bless them every one.

Forget hoop-skirted Jo March, stern Queen Victoria with her perfect little Christmas tree, and the burping Roman Bacchus. Let us go back to the infant Jesus and, long before him, to the unnamed millions who watched for the sun's return at the time of the winter solstice. This is an important time for those of us who fumble around for a concept of Christian humanism. Well, I may have just pushed a panic button with the "h" word. Humanism was around a long time before televangelists identified it as the evil of the age. For many of us, the word does not conjure up militant atheists fighting religious fanatics with tracts and law suits, but suggests Renaissance scholars and artists becoming free of dogma and examining their culture, secular and sacred, from a human and critical perspective. There have been examples of Christian humanists from at least Erasmus (1466–1536) and Thomas More (1478–1535), those men of all seasons, down to contemporary pathfinders like the Protestant activist-theologian-martyr Dietrich Bonhoeffer (1906–1945) and the progressive Catholic ecumenist, Hans Küng (1928–). Southern novelist Walker Percy (1916–1990) was a leading writer in the Catholic branch of this Christian humanist tradition. Now stay with me, this really is related to the winter solstice.

Percy's novels often begin with the human quest for the sacred rather than from God's own manifestations. Religious critics say that humanists, like Percy, become obsessed with the journey rather than the destination. I don't see anything wrong with that. I think what really troubles traditionalists is that, in addition to people who arrive at faith from revelations of God, made personally or in traditions of faith, there are also people whose Christian faith is based on an exploration of the human condition — looking for holiness in being itself. Occasionally the humanistic process can turn weird, but the sacred is still delightfully in there somewhere. In Percy's *Love in the Ruins*[5] we find a man named after Thomas More on his patio on Christmas day after Mass, wearing sackcloth while barbecuing. He alternates between singing popular songs and Latin chants before carrying his wife to bed — "where all good folk belong." People in pre-Roman times would have understood what this twentieth-century Catholic humanist was expressing. The experience of most Catholic humanists is much less colorful.

When I think of the winter solstice today I imagine hilltops. Many years ago I lived near the northern shore of San Francisco Bay and worked in the city. It was an exciting time when many people were actively reexamining their assumptions about life. Something in that time of openness led me to suggest to friends that we gather to watch the dawn on the day of the winter solstice. Almost all agreed. There may have been a mutual desire to escape the "only four more shopping days until Christmas!" mentality in the city.

So it was that about twenty people arrived at my house in the dark with blankets and thermos bottles. We walked up a nearby hill and sat in silence, looking at the stars. The spiritual types probably prayed or meditated. I did. The freethinkers just thought freely. In time the sun began to rise over the East Bay hills. Eventually we stood up and left. The suggestion was made that we do this the next year. And we did, every year until I moved away. Why? No one ever put it into words. It was simply a very authentic moment. Our time together was the same experience for all of us and a very different experience for each of us.

In these present days of sometimes painful cultural divide, I think back to our annual gatherings on that hill. We were atheists, Buddhists, Christians, and Jews as well as those who considered themselves ex-atheists, ex-Buddhists, ex-Christians, and ex-Jews. There were some whom today we would call Evangelicals and New Agers. Some sitting there were working for radical political change. Others were convinced that change had to come from inside each person. Some wore suits during the day and others wore beads. We came up the hill from many different life directions. Yet we shared a moment together in which we somehow touched with others who had stood on other hills for thousands of years before us. Although we were very different from one another, we supported each other in our individual searches for the sacred.

Times change. I don't always go out to greet the dawn on the day of the winter solstice But I think I would be better for it if I did.

22

HOLY PLACES

STONES ARE SACRED. Ancient people piled them in mounds to mark holy meeting places. Their descendants learned to fashion them into temples. Other descendants sometimes tore the structures down in an attempt to destroy the soul of a people.

Romans destroyed Jerusalem's great temple in 70 CE following a Jewish revolt. The only thing left is the Western Wall. It is a retaining wall that supports a hill known as the Temple Mount, which is sacred to Muslims, Jews, and Christians. The wall, sometimes called the Wailing Wall, is constructed of magnificent stones from many time periods. It was said to be near the western wall of the what was the Temple's Holy of Holys, from which the Divine Presence has never departed, according to some Jewish traditions. It is easy to believe that. I was there on a day when Muslim militants up on the mount were fighting Israeli militants down below. Yet along the wall there was peace. We all had our personal reason for being there. I, like most, touched the stones and let them speak to me. On my left, a boy from Eastern Europe was having his Bar Mitzvah. On his other side an elderly Christian peace activist from Akron, Ohio was crying. On my right, a young man in a black fur hat was praying and bowing. Next to him was an atheist friend of mine from England pushing a note from her grandmother into a crack between the stones. What was I doing while leaning on those stones? Just being there and feeling the presence of God, of history, of my own life. When I left the wall, someone from Asia took my place. And so it has been, and will be, for centuries. Stones are sacred, at least to me. Nature or people can destroy a building but not the stones.

For most of the time religious structures today are empty — stones defining a space consecrated to something important but always unknown and mysterious. Getting caught in a sudden shower is an excuse to duck into an empty church. And if nature doesn't cooperate, it can always look as if it might rain. I find it easy to feel at home in abandoned chapels that dot the countryside in Europe. It is a bit harder in an American city where some denomination is marking a church with the signs of its proprietorship, but we shouldn't let that discourage a quiet visit. No one has ever truly owned the stones. Places are made sacred by what happens there. Entering a church, I am aware of several parallel worlds. There is the one you can read about in the church bulletin and the unseen, but palpable, one that is the convergence of so many journeys. Countless people, like myself, have found a quiet spiritual oasis in a church for a few moments. Thousands have hopped along religious stepping stones in any church; christenings, communions, marriages, funerals. Personal experiences of joy and sorrow have been better understood, or at least endured, by something indefinable in these places. Oh, people have walked out in disgust. I have done that also. But that is in the other world — the official, church bulletin veneer. In the still space between the stone walls, there is almost always something deep.

A child's intuitive sense of the sacred often helps us understand spiritual fundamentals. When my daughter, Holly, was almost seven, a fatally ill infant came into her life. We all knew the child would die, but it was a shock when it happened. Holly

received the news one morning as she was setting out to school. She told me that we would need to do something before she could go to school. "We have to go to a place where people pray," she announced. I walked her to a nearby Catholic church where a Mass was in process and asked if this would do. "No," she said, "we have to wait 'til the priest leaves." In the after-service silence of that space, Holly somehow came to terms with the death. I think she also said good-bye. After a while Holly told me, "We can light a candle and leave now." We did. I learned that day that every church has a Western Wall.

When I walk up the steps of an impressive, yet ignored, city church, I sometimes think of Hermann Hesse's (1877–1962) reflection when coming upon a small rose-red chapel while exploring an Italian-Swiss region: "Oh, beloved, intimate chapels of this country! You bear the signs and inscriptions of a god who is not mine. Your believers utter words I do not know. And yet I can still pray in you just as well as in the oak forest or in the mountain meadow.... To you, every prayer is acceptable and holy."[6]

But how does one pray in such circumstances? Hesse suggests that we simply recount our condition. Which, I think, translates into an honest quest for the holy ground in each of us. We should, as Hesse puts it, sing forth our sufferings and our thanks — "as little children sing."

So what is the point here? During this season we can, and hopefully do, become more aware of our individual journeys. It is also good to see our path as one among many. Temples, mosques, and churches are all places constructed to be crossroads of spiritual paths. Many voices still whisper in the quiet of holy places. Sitting alone in a no longer used Shaker meetinghouse in Massachusetts, I sensed that the intensity of their worship had been so strong that it would be centuries before the echo of songs, dances, and prayers died away. We have all had experiences like that in great basilicas and humble shrines, or just walking among stones in an open field on a path many have trod before.

Sometime in this season, it would be good to let each of our stories become one of the many to be found within the sacred space of a holy place.

23

BIRDS

WHEN MY MOTHER COULD no longer put up her own Christmas tree, she gave me a small box of her remaining ornaments. Amidst the faded and chipped balls was a bird made of bright red felt, which clipped onto a branch. It has become "Grandma's cardinal" to my children. The cardinal was for my mother, and many others of her age, a powerful symbol of Christmas. Why? It is a bird well adapted to the cold. The flash of red against nature's grey or white background is striking. But there is something more. In the middle of life's storms, a red bird has often been a sign of hope. While on a solitary wilderness retreat, Paula D'Arcy encountered such a red bird. She loved its song and the sight of it in the wasteland. Her reflective life was suddenly disrupted by a tornado, forcing her to take shelter in an abandoned bunkhouse until the violence subsided. "As I am about to step out, a flash of color at my foot startles me, and I look down. There on the doorstep, waiting, is the red bird. Tears spill from my eyes and I can barely breathe.... The storm was one display of power. His waiting for me, another. Such a moment is a gift."[7]

We don't have cardinals where I live on the West Coast of the United States, but I have come to value any bird at this time of year. When I am focused on some difficulty, in my life or in the weather, I often can look out the window and see a bird with a different perspective on the existence we are sharing at the moment. It is not only that she can fly and I cannot. We have common basic needs, which I approach in complicated ways and she with simplicity. She eats, finds shelter, breeds in a natural way. And when she dies, which I am told will probably be in a violent fashion, she will exhibit the same grace. The end is not something that concerns her. It does me. Life is what the bird sings about and what I want to more fully appreciate — up to my last breath.

Gratitude for life enters in here somewhere. That is what St. Francis was explaining to the birds one day. He and his brothers had been walking along when Francis saw a great multitude of birds. Telling his companions to rest, he went over and preached to the birds. His main point was that they should be aware of the sin of ingratitude. I wonder whether any complaining brothers were also listening? Francis reminded his little winged sisters and brothers that, although they did not "spin nor sew," they had clothing, water, food, and all they needed for a happy life. Therefore at all times and in every place, they should sing God's praise. The birds, and I suspect the brothers, seemed to understand. At least the birds around our farm appear grateful to be participating in the unfolding of creation.

We all come up against difficulties in life, and sometimes they seem more formidable during the winter months. It is natural to turn and attempt to escape a painful predicament. But it doesn't work. Our only satisfying path lies, somehow, in walking into the storm. Where there is sorrow from a great loss, or frustration from failing to live up to our expectations of ourselves, we are better off to embrace the very thing causing us the pain. At least four centuries ago, some musician in Gascony looked to the birds of marsh and mountain for an example. The "Carol of the Birds" begins, in one version, with "Whence comes this rush of wings afar. . . . " These vulnerable little creatures choose to come out into fierce winter storms to encounter the essence of life as symbolized in the humble birth of Jesus. Some versions of the carol list the birds. The lyric songs of the nightingale and finch mix with the hoarse chants of the magpie and raven. The magnificent eagle soars above the pudgy partridge. Everyone has a place in this "wondrous flight." The image reminds me of times when we all find ourselves facing formidable cliffs in life. We are all different. Yet at a moment of extreme frustration, we are all capable of flying.

I have never heard a "rush of wings" on Christmas Eve. But I have witnessed wondrous flights at other times of year. Swallows that winter in South America migrate to our farm in the spring. They build nests and raise their young. Once, in August, a barn they favored burned down, killing many of them. The next year a few, who had been born at our place, found their way back. In a few years the flock was up to size again. They arrive in small groups and begin at once to make their nests under the eaves and then lay eggs. At sunrise and sunset they fill the air, catching insects for themselves and their newborn. Then comes a day in late summer when they make great circles over the farm. I suspect they are testing to see whether all the young birds will be able to fly the many thousands of miles on their migration. I also like to imagine they are saying good-bye and "See you next year!" It is a great sight. And then they are gone. I watched this spectacle recently on the day I received some news from a doctor that was less than what I had hoped for. I compared the days, weeks, and months that I would face with tests and cures with what those little birds were going to endure before they could have peace again in a familiar place. It helped put my own disappointment into perspective. I would think of the hardships they were enduring and the courage they were exhibiting as I experienced unfamiliar and unwanted things that autumn.

These days in the heart of winter are good times to look for birds in our backyards or the trees that line our streets. They are there, and these little creatures bring with them grace, and hope, and sometimes a song — if we will take the time to listen.

24

TINA'S TEA

THESE ARE DAYS, and nights, for sitting by the fire and hearing again parts of the long chronicle of human existence. The tales that have been handed down to us only have meaning when they connect with our individual experiences. And there are sacred stories in every person's life, and in every household, that need to be added to past lore. Everything we ponder, and remember, on these days reflects some aspect of what matters most to us. Our thoughts do not always unfold in a deep and solemn way; sometimes it is humorous when we think about meetings of the divine and the human.

St. Luke's story of the first Christmas Eve is repeated many times each year. It is a good story, but I doubt things happened exactly the way we are told. Among other things, the sheep bother me. We read that there were shepherds watching their flocks when *the angel of the Lord appeared to them and the glory of the Lord shone around them*. There also appeared *a throng of the heavenly host* singing away. What were the sheep doing all this time? The ones I see in fields around our farm start running when a rabbit hops along. If they saw a great firework display of the *glory of the Lord* and were confronted with a clamoring *throng of the heavenly host*, they would bolt over hill and dale with the shepherds chasing after them. No one would have made it to Bethlehem that night. So I think it is best to forget the details and look at Luke's point. Simple, poor, humble, close-to-the-earth folks got to the child quickly and understood what was happening.

com-
and
ons.

ake
he
ut
ul
s
h

...ity, wise, rich, sweet-smelling crowd was so ...selves they didn't have a clue about was go- ...from life's storms was at that simple crib, not ...wealth and power.

...eve it took heavenly guidance to get the shep- ...rib. Somehow they had to stop thinking about ...ice of wool, girlfriends, and a good meal for a ...i, and in that empty space they had to be open to ...ty that there might be something of great signifi- ...e little things around them. Such as a light coming ...ole. I think that is the constant wonder of Christmas ...ignore the big things long enough to encounter the ...oments. One of our family's memories has become an ...g liturgy in our lives, reenacted each Christmas Eve. It ...many years ago.[8]

...na was born with AIDS in 1988. In those days there were ...life-extending options. A caring and very ill young woman ...d us to be with her when she gave birth to Tina and to adopt ...r. There are three adults, and parents, in our family — Julie, ...Marti, and myself. We have been spiritual companions for many years. Our life with Tina was so joyful and powerful that we are still living with her, even though she died just before her third birthday. Everyone experienced different facets of Tina. Julie described her this way: "Tina was happy and sure of herself, cute and charming, a bright whimsical pixie, who made every day delightful. . . . She was always ready for celebrations, which she called 'happies.'"[9]

As her last Christmas approached, things were often not very happy for Tina, or us. Her immune system had collapsed. The infections were unrelenting and painful. On the day of Christmas Eve Tina became very ill. Julie and Marti rushed her to the hospital, a trip of about two hours from our farm. Late in the

afternoon Marti called me. It looked very bad. Tina was
fortable but might not last the night. I put down the phone
turned around to face the other children and their questi
What was going to happen with Tina and with Christmas?

The high point of our Christmas Eve is when we each t
a lantern and walk quietly up the hill to our little chapel. T
kids and I did it that night, with the help of two friends. B
there was, for me, considerable tension between this peacef
moment and my personal grief. I realized this might be Tina
last night of life, and yet there was a need to celebrate the birth
of new life with the other children. They went to bed with peace
and expectations for the morning. At the hospital Tina was in
a deep sleep.

Marti, Julie, and I were on the phone later when the old farm
clock tolled midnight. We read together a favorite passage from
the Bible (Wisdom 18:14):

> When peaceful silence lay over all,
> and night had run the half of her swift course,
> down from the heavens, from the royal throne,
> leapt your all-powerful word. . . .

We wished each other a blessed Christmas and prayed for Tina
and all those other families keeping watch over their children
that night. In her backpack Julie had a little bottle of Grand
Marnier purchased for an eggnog that was never made. There
were no glasses in the room. But for some reason Tina's favorite
toy tea set had come with her to the hospital. Solemnly, standing
on either side of Tina, Julie and Marti poured the liqueur into
the tiny cups and drank a toast.

Surprisingly Tina recovered the next day, and with a little
pushing against normal procedure, left the hospital. It was a

sweet and simple Christmas day. Our family was reunited for a few more precious months.

On every Christmas Eve we gather around the hearth at 2:00 p.m., which is midnight in Bethlehem. Whatever seasonal tasks are not done at that point are to remain undone! Lists are thrown away. Christmas begins. We light a fire, using the trunk of last year's tree and, like many others on this day, sing songs and share memories. At some point, Julie brings out Tina's prized tea set and Marti produces a bottle of Grand Marnier. In the following moments we again feel the presence of Tina and all who have been an important part of our life, and our Christmases. We share reflections about the homeless family in Bethlehem and all the families under stress in our own times. At some point a holy quiet envelops us. Time ceases to exist, and we know we rest on sacred ground.

Then, like Christmas bells, the children jubilantly bring out special treats, and for the first of many times we embrace each other with hopes for a happy and blessed Christmas. It is a party at which some guests are only present with us in spirit — but we are together. It is that connection with the past and the present, and perhaps the future, but most of all with each other, which I hope is present in every home where people gather on this day.

25

THE CHRISTMAS COMPANY

W<small>HO HAS ANY CONTROL</small> over Christmas day? Up early. Stockings. Presents. Tons of wrapping paper. Happy mess. Frantic cleanup. Relatives and friends on the way. Toys not working as planned. No batteries. Tears. Big dinner. Eggnog. Too much to drink. Time to read *A Child's Christmas in Wales*. Book can't be found. And so on. Is it any wonder we are often relieved when the day is over?

What if the day brings together people who grate on each other? The shadows can be heavy. In 1931, a time of economic and political tension in the world, Eduardo de Filippo, the renowned Neopolitan actor and playwright, presented a play in which a dysfunctional family rapidly unraveled on Christmas day.[10] While this is happening, the father focuses all his interest and energy on the seemingly childish activity of constructing a *presepe*, the traditional tabletop nativity scene, much to his family's irritation. In the end, the father has a stroke, and in that changed environment his simplicity leads the family back to what is really important. Maybe it is possible to do the same thing without the stroke and, for that matter, without anyone knowing what we are doing.

Here is my covert plan. I think there is a whole theater company inside each of us. Many different characters dialogue with each other continually — although we often deny it. "That wasn't me arguing with myself in the shower. It must have been the radio." Well, Christmas is the day to put our inner actors to work. The play, or tableau, is a living *presepe* but with some unusual characters mixed in with the traditional ones. Now who might play Mary, Joseph, Jesus, a farmer, the innkeeper and so on? Each of us will have a different cast for our play. Does this strike you as mental role-playing, or a medieval mystery play? It doesn't matter how you see it. To me, it is a theatrical performance on the stage of our inner world.

The way this works is that once we have our characters and have given them a little guidance, they will stand by in the wings until we call them forth. For example, in the "real" world, outside me, Aunt Maude has just made her third snide comment about cousin Beaufort's wife. I assume an ambiguous stance and send out the call, inside me, for the innkeeper to enter, stage right. What would be going on with him? His priorities were financial gain and so he turned Mary and Joseph away. But now that the baby is born perhaps there are regrets. It has become his habit to judge everything by the financial bottom line. There is something very special about a new life coming into this world. Perhaps I have him in dialogue with Joseph. And so it goes. By the time the innkeeper exits stage left on my interior stage, Aunt Maude has exited in a huff to find a little brandy. Need another example? There is total chaos in the kitchen. Something is burning. The whole day is going to be ruined. "Can I help?" "No, just keep out of the way." The kids are playing with their toys. I sit down and fix my eyes as if I were watching. And another act begins inside me. The farmer who owns the animals in the stable is coming to find out what is going on and encounters a Buddhist sage from the East. What do these events mean to a wise man who does not refer to a personal god and to a simple man who only knows the earth and the seasons? Well, you are probably getting the picture. All through the day I find moments to pop in on my *presepe*. It brings me a sense of balance and lets me enter more fully into the hectic festivities.

Who are some of my characters? The cast always seems to start with Joseph the carpenter. And the script goes something like this: "I am a man of dreams. I look at a piece of wood, and I see what I can make from it. I looked at Mary, and I could see her as my wife, the mother of my children. My children — my future. The boys will all work with me. My daughters will dance around the workshop, getting in the way, running off to help their mother, leaving behind their laughter. My home is my world. I made a table. I could see all my family gathered around it for the Sabbath meal, week after week for years to come.

"But things have not gone as I dreamed. After we were engaged but before we were married, Mary became pregnant. Half the town thought I had taken advantage of her. The other half wanted to stone her. Mary is different from my family and neighbors. She hears things and sees things no one else hears or sees. She hints that God is calling her for something special.

"I wanted to marry Mary. I loved her. She would make my home fresh and bright. But the child! To bring Mary to my home as my wife would be saying, 'I am the father of this child.' I come from a respectable family. We descended from King David. I could not bring shame on our name. Yet that was exactly what I wanted to do.

"Then came the dream. I heard a voice. 'Be not afraid,' it said. The voice said to take Mary home as my wife. 'She has conceived what is in her by the spirit of God.' I woke up with a great feeling of peace. That very day I gathered some friends and took Mary home in marriage. She cried and she laughed. But my family was divided. My sanctimonious Uncle Aaron led a crowd to my house. He said Mary was shameful and unbalanced and this marriage blackened the reputation of the House of David. My father, Jacob, stood up for us. He reminded Aaron that David had slept with Bathsheba and saw to it that her husband was killed. That he took Abishag, a young girl, to his bed 'to keep him warm.' He shouted that we should be talking about 'love' not 'shame' because it was David's love of God that distinguished him. As to Mary not being normal, what about Elisha finding God, not in the mighty wind, not in the earthquake, not in the fire, but in the gentle breeze. He said Mary is a girl who listens to gentle breezes. Well, Uncle Aaron ripped his shirt over the sacrilege of comparing Mary to the prophets. Then he and his followers went away. All this time Mary was behind me, hanging on to me and crying. Later my father came to me and said it might be better if Mary and I left town until the child was born.

"I sold the house and the table I had made. The table of my dreams. I bought a donkey and put what things we had on him. The days were quite cold now. We walked slowly as Mary was very large. Along the way she started having trouble. I unloaded the donkey and put her on him. Some of our things I left by the road. The rest I carried. I am a person who likes to plan things out. Yet here we were wandering, often cold, sometimes wet, with no home and little money. But we were happy. And the happiness seemed to grow as we traveled along the road. Mary's thoughts were all on the child, but I had to think ahead — to provide for them.

"Yesterday morning Mary told me that she thought her time was close. As the day wore on it was obvious that she was right. This surprised us both. There were problems I had to solve and fast. I had to find shelter, food, and a midwife. There is still much to do, but one thought pounded in my brain. My child, yes my child, is going to be born and all our lives will be changed forever."

Mary is always a silent character for me. Sometimes I have a young Mary and an old Mary encounter each other in my mind. She was probably about sixteen when Jesus was born and about fifty when he was brutalized and executed. She may have lived for a long time after that and I feel that in her the young Mary and the old Mary found ways of comforting each other. The wonder and beauty of that first night with her son, that night of his birth, would help to heal the soul-sickness in seeing the child she raised crushed so viciously. Of course, death was not the final word for Jesus. But even Easter joy could not erase a mother's pain.

There are so many characters that the company within each of us can play. As I age, an old couple appears more regularly in my cast. They come out of a legend, from Provence I think. After traveling to the manger, with great difficulty, they were told they would be granted one wish. They discussed it between themselves. Each year those discussions go to deeper and deeper levels for me. What was it they actually asked for? That they might die on the same day.

The angels are always good for comic relief when things get a little solemn in my play. An interior angelic voice once reflected on the shepherds, and the rest of humanity, this way: "Shepherds are a rough, crude lot by nature. But they do understand the stars. Look at the heavens night after night and you will feel a tug. After all, you humans were formed out of stardust. Well, I managed to get the souls of the shepherds emptied of plodding things. Then those souls just lifted up, and it was easy for them to experience something of the phenomenal awe of that night. And it is an ongoing event. Get it? The Holy Night is prolonged into every night — every birth. This night. Your birth."

Then followed an angelic frustration about how humans are so slow to grasp that God is to be found in the ordinary moments of life, concluding with an admonition: "It would help if you would watch the margins of your life. As you are racing somewhere to do something supposedly important, a person you rush by could be involved in the most significant event on earth at that moment. Think about it! And for heavens sake, if you feel one of us pushing you, don't be so resistant. It can be very tiring! We are not as young as we were you know. It really would help if you took a bit more responsibility in these matters. [*Angel disappears in blaze of glory.*]"

At some point, late on Christmas day, the domestic world and my inner theater might come together. Enthusiasm for new things begins to wane. Tempos slow down. If there is any sense of required joviality, it has worn thin. It is the time for random suggestions. I usually start with the young people, who are more tolerant of me. I ask one, "What would the shepherd boy be thinking on the first Christmas?" And to another, "If you were a servant girl sent over from the inn with a blanket, how would you react to all this?" In time most people join in the action. Tragedy, history, and comedy overlap rather freely for a little while.

Then the play fades away. As does the day.

26

THE SECOND DAY

HEY, STOP PACKING UP the ornaments. Christmas isn't over. It is just beginning! This is St. Stephen's Day, the second of the Twelve Days of Christmas. In medieval times festivities filled all these days. Armies were forbidden to fight. Harsh nature made farming impossible. Frankly, people needed a midwinter break. We still do. It would be a shame to stop everything at the end of Christmas day.

Meanwhile, at the mall, the holiday decorations are coming down, customers are exchanging unwanted gifts, and stores are discounting their unpurchased inventory while cutting back on staff and hours. Precisely because the commercial world moves into a slower gear, the days following Christmas are a unique facet of the season. I find that if I simply avoid stores, the Christmas season naturally flows on as it did centuries before there were malls.

In recent years an increasing number of my friends have found ways to prolong Christmastime. Some go until the new year and others all the way to January 5, the evening before Epiphany, Twelfth Night. My family usually makes it up to my birthday on January 4. A few people I know take off to the ski slopes. Most of us are lucky just to have a long weekend at this time. Then it is back to our normal daytime activity. It is a matter of attitude more than anything else. To me, the week after December 25 is not the time after Christmas. It is Christmastime. I look forward to unhurriedly experiencing all the things I could never cram into December 25 which is only the first day of Christmas.

For my family, like most families celebrating Ramadan, Chanukah, or Kwanzaa,[11] the evening meal is the special focus of the day. Around the table we take pleasure in each other and the season. There is time to explore what it means for each of us. There is an opportunity here for everyone with children in their lives. If December 25 was a little too much "it is all about me," the following day is a chance to change the tempo and think of others. It is an old tradition. In many countries belonging to the British Commonwealth, December 26 is Boxing Day. Often it means giving gifts to service people, but originally it referred to opening the church Poor Box and distributing the contents to those in need. Presumably, well-off parishioners leaving services on Christmas day, with the choir extolling good deeds, would be moved to drop in a contribution.

The carol in my head on this day after Christmas is "Good King Wenceslas" which I catch myself humming. The king looked out of his castle window on December 26, the feast of St. Stephen, "when a poor man came in sight." Page and monarch left their own revels and went off to bring warmth and food to the fellow.[12] John Mason Neale (1818–1866), an Anglican clergyman who directed a home for the poor, wrote the words of the carol. The last stanza puts forth the central theme for this day:

> Therefore, Christian men, be sure,
> Wealth or rank possessing,
> Ye who now will bless the poor,
> Shall yourselves find blessing.

Singing the carol is a community event around our hearth. All but the very young males sing the part of the king. And all the girls, women, and small boys sing the page. The narration is sung together. But "Christian men" becomes "Christians all," and woe to the young fellow who laments that he hates to sing with the girls!

After the long carol is sung, talk naturally turns to concerns about equality, poverty, justice, and personal responsibility for doing something about them. Wenceslas can still disturb our consciences on the feast of Stephen. Once, when the suggestion was made for the family to send a donation over to a homeless shelter, one of the teenagers challenged us. "That is not what Wenceslas did!" she thundered. And she was right. Wenceslas got out and shared the experience of the cold as he walked the distance to the man's house. Entering into the human condition of people in stress often means more to them than the help we bring. Friends of ours had it right when their family helped prepare and serve a holiday meal at a senior center.

I rarely get away with quoting scripture to make a point, but the man whose birthday we just celebrated did say (Luke 14:12–13): "When you give a lunch or dinner, do not ask your friends, brothers, relations or rich neighbors, for fear they repay your courtesy by inviting you in return. No; when you have a party, invite the poor, the crippled, the lame, the blind...."

Well, should we give it a try?

27

SKYROCKET

THE ONLY TIME my father set fire to a neighbor's roof was
on Christmas Eve when I was eight.

Picayune, Mississippi, is the town of my birth. It was founded
in 1904 and named by the owner of the *Times-Picayune,* a newspaper in nearby New Orleans. Who knows what was on her
mind. In older times, a "picayune" was the smallest coin in use
in this part of the South. It was an embarrassment to the few
prominent families that the town was labeled as a place of little
significance. Most working people, if they considered it at all,
thought it rather apt.

Our county, Pearl River, had more black people than white
ones. In Picayune, they lived east of the railroad tracks, and we
whites were on the west side. Our schools had lights, indoor
plumbing, and floors. Their schools did not. But this tale is not
about racial issues, except that they put a distance between my
father and most other men in the town. Dad was not militant,
but he was firm in his views on equality. This was a region where
some blacks were mistreated and even lynched. Occasionally,
before matters got really serious, my father would disrupt an
ugly scene with his dry wit and good humor. Despite being out
of step on a very fundamental social issue, he was well-respected
and popular with people in the town.

When my parents moved to Picayune in 1929, they brought
some customs that were alien to our neighbors. At Christmas

we shot off fireworks. This came from my mother's great-grandfather's time in Virginia. People of his day had memories of Christmas day in Europe that included the thunderous pealing of many church bells. There were few church bells in rural Virginia, but there were a few cannons and lots of fireworks, those little Chinese toys Europeans have used for celebrations since Marco Polo brought some to Venice. To be honest, my father never needed any historical justification. He simply liked to set off fireworks at Christmas.

I remember my father as a quiet man. He was on the edge of most gatherings, but his gentle smile gave a sense of calm to the moment. He was a peace-loving man, quite different from his brother, who later became a high sheriff in a neighboring state. The story was told of my uncle, at ten, being bested in a fight with the girl next door. He shouted to my Dad, "Bring the ax!" My father, all of eight, decided to brave the wrath of a big brother and chose the path of nonviolence. On reflection, it is surprising that this mellow person would take such delight in Christmas explosions.

Times were hard for us, and for the whole area, in the late 1930s. Dad worked at the local lumber mill, and we lived in a rented company house surrounded by other mill families. Like them we bought food at the store owned by the mill. Workers were partially paid in scrip to be used at that store. People could be fired for shopping anyplace else. The account that many people ran up at the store was often a little more than they had scrip to pay for. There was a trapped feeling among workers in the best of times, and these were depression years with many families suffering from poverty. By common consent, Christmas was a time to put away your fears for the future and enjoy each other. The time I remember best was Christmas Eve in 1939.

At sundown most of our neighbors gathered in their kitchens for a Christmas Eve supper. The McBee family was our nearest neighbor, just beyond our garden and chicken house. They were listening to their new radio. Nelson Eddy's voice could be heard singing whenever their door opened to admit one of their many relatives.

While families around us were sitting down at their tables, Dad collected us in the darkening backyard beside a large tin washtub. He placed a number of firecrackers under the inverted tub. In the enclosed metallic hollow, any sound would be magnified. Finding a way to make the most of what you had was a talent that all depression-era parents developed. The firecrackers were connected on strips. After a while, Dad got a little carried away. He lit all the remaining strips and threw them under the tub together. The resulting heat caused all the firecrackers to go off at once. The tub shot up into the air, with a deafening explosion. Geese and chickens awoke and squawked in terror. The overall effect was quite pleasing to an eight year old.

After many firecrackers, sparklers, and Roman candles, Dad produced his favorite device — a giant skyrocket that one of his fishing partners had made. Always a very cautious person, Dad warned us back a good ten feet before jamming the wooden shaft deep into the red Mississippi earth. Then he lit the rocket's fuse. We knew something was wrong when Dad motioned us to get even farther away. The rocket was stuck and instead of exploding up in the air would likely blow up right in our backyard. We ran behind the woodpile to watch. The fuse had almost burned up when the rocket slowly rose a few inches off the ground. I can still hear the "hzzzz" and feel the excitement of the impending destruction of the backyard. Suddenly, the rocket climbed to the height of the persimmon tree, picked up speed, turned, and made straight for the McBees' roof.

Nelson Eddy was just swinging into "O Little Town of Beth-lehem" when the rocket hit the roof. There was a flash of blue, and a shingle ignited. After a few seconds, the fire activated the rocket and it exploded, sending multicolored stars all over the roof and cascading to the ground. None of the people in the house were aware of this extraordinary sight.

My father went into our house for his big jacket and a bucket. He opened the backyard gate and walked very deliberately over to the McBee house. There was no sense of panic. It was as if he was returning a pail of something borrowed. Above him the flames slowly spread. Dad stepped onto their small porch and knocked on the front door. The radio was loud and they did not hear him. He knocked again. Mr. McBee, a large man who tended to drink a bit too much, appeared and embraced my father. Dad was invited in. We could see him trying to explain but being shoved inside by our jovial neighbor.

For a long moment, all was still. We were motionless, watch-ing the McBee's empty porch and the flames on their roof. Then the front door flew open, and the McBee family poured out, yelling. Mrs. McBee emerged last, carrying the new radio. Other neighbors, alerted by the clamor, gathered by the side of the house. A ladder was produced. My father filled his bucket at the pump and passed it up a chain of excited friends. Five times the bucket went up and down before the flames were extinguished. Someone brought down what was left of the burned-out rocket, and everyone looked at my father. Soon the air was filled with laughter. Mr. McBee ran in the house for a bottle, which was passed around. By the time Dad started home, he had become the man of the hour for having provided a unique Christmas Eve.

Christmas was on a Monday that year. On the next Satur-day night, Mrs. McBee invited us over to listen to the radio. My mother brought some of her justly famous fruitcake. I had never heard a radio except from a distance. The McBees had never tasted fruitcake. We listened to the war news from Europe. Mrs. McBee asked for the fruitcake recipe. Then we walked home. I looked up at my father. He had a broad smile. Life for the whole world was about to change, but that was a Christmas I will never forget.

28

RACHEL'S CHILDREN

I T WAS A BRIGHT, but troubled, September morning in 2000 when I visited the Children's Memorial at Yad Vashem, the national center for Holocaust remembrance near Jerusalem. Earlier a friend had seen an Arab schoolboy thrown against an iron gate in a renewed skirmish with security forces in the old city. The boy was bleeding. Big trouble was brewing. You could feel it in the air. It is not so odd for me to remember that Jerusalem morning during Christmas week. December 28 is designated in many church calendars as the Feast of the Holy Innocents.

Matthew's gospel tells the story of the magi coming to King Herod for help finding the infant "king of the Jews." Herod did not want any rivals for that title. When his priests told him of prophecies that the messiah was to be born in Bethlehem, he sent troops to kill all the male children under the age of two in the region. Then Matthew quotes a poignant verse from the prophet Jeremiah (31:15):

> A voice was heard in Ramah,
> sobbing and loudly lamenting:
> it was Rachel weeping for her children,
> refusing to be comforted
> because they were no more.

Look, I don't know if this really happened. I rather think it didn't, but I do know that many wholly innocent children have been slaughtered during my lifetime and it is good to remember

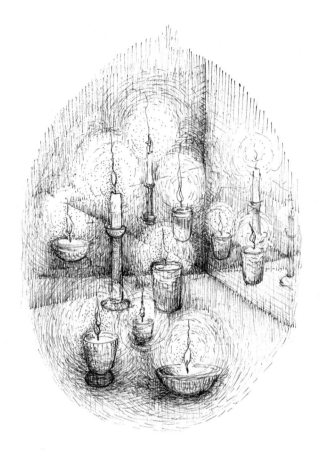

them at this time of year. One child I knew, dying from AIDS, told her family to "remember me at parties." We have lit so many candles during this season, it won't hurt to light another for the children we miss.

The Children's Memorial at Yad Vashem is hollowed out of an underground cavern. As I moved from the bright sunlight into a dark place, I thought it a good expression of what happens when a child's naturally bright future is extinguished. Groping my way along, I began to hear names. One and a half million

Jewish children perished in the Holocaust. How many more children died in the bombing of cities on all sides in that war? And it still goes on. War today is not limited to warrior against warrior. It is more often warrior against civilian. In recent years 90 percent of the casualties in an armed conflict are civilian, and half of those are children. Two million children have perished in the conflicts of the past decade.[13] There is no way to avoid such slaughter once a modern war machine starts rolling.

A recording of children's names filled the darkness, and grew louder as I edged along the path. A name. The age at which the child was murdered. His or her country of origin. Then another name. What about the unnamed? The unknown children we failed to protect in so many ways. Their voices are somehow also in this darkness.

Many of the children whose names I heard were born the year I was born — 1931. There is a story behind each name.

Eva, eleven, The Netherlands. Her father was a school teacher. The family was totally integrated in the life of their small city. When the Germans came, Eva's parents sent her to live with a Christian family in the country. Several years later she was turned in for a reward, deported to Auschwitz, and murdered on arrival.

Monia, ten, Lithuania. His grandparents had a farm near his small village. When the Germans came, his family had to leave their home and live in an overcrowded ghetto with little food, medicine, or sanitation. One day he was marched out into the country, made to stand along a big ditch, and shot by the *Einsatzgruppen*, a special mobile killing squad.

Oro, twelve, Greece. Her family ran a clothing store in Salonica, where many Jews had settled after being expelled from Spain in 1492. When Greece was defeated in 1941, the Germans took their store, and the family had no way to earn a living. Later Oro's home was surrounded and everyone thrown out violently, including her father who could not walk because of a recent stroke. They were pushed, with eighty others, into a cattle car with three barrels. One barrel held olives, one water, and one served as a toilet. Each person was given a loaf of bread. A month later they arrived at Auschwitz. A week later Oro was murdered.

Baroukh-Raoul, thirteen, Algeria. After his father and two brothers died in a death camp, Baroukh was sent to live at a children's home in the French countryside. It was pleasant until Klaus Barbie, the "Butcher of Lyon," arrived one morning with three vans and took all the children and the staff away. The kids were between four and thirteen. Baroukh was murdered at Auschwitz just after his thirteenth birthday.

Baroukh, Oro, Monia, Eva, and I could have been in the same class at school, and all I know about them is how they were murdered. Did Eva love to dance and party like other Dutch girls her age? Did Monia hike the countryside with friends? Did Oro sing or play the fiddle at festivals? Did Baroukh have a passion for sports?

As I walked along, I saw a light flicker. It looked like a single candle, maybe several, I couldn't tell. I entered a very large room with a ceiling several stories high. There were mirrors and glass everywhere. It was arranged so images of candles were reflected anyplace I looked. Waves of candle flames filled the room. The names went on. I paused to understand — the names, the dark, the burning candle images. In my heart I heard a whisper: "Remember me."

These were Jewish children killed by people who considered themselves Christian. Some of the children, like Eva, probably didn't think of themselves as Jewish, yet they became Jewish martyrs. We must all respect the uniqueness of this grief. But for me, that morning in Jerusalem transcended even that great Jewish lament. It is wrong for any child to be killed in any war, for any reason. As I relive that morning at the Children's Memorial, in my heart I hear other names from newspapers and letters.

Amina, eleven, Sudan. She was in a hospital in Darfur when it was bombed in an air raid.

Dzems, ten, Bosnia. He was caught in crossfire when shopping with his mother.

Hakim, ten, Iraq. He was killed by a suicide bomber while taking candy from an American soldier.

Nouran, ten, Gaza. She was shot by a soldier in a guard-station when she came out of school for recess.

Noor, ten, Afghanistan. He was killed in his house when it was bombed from the air, following Sunday dinner.

Sadako, twelve, Japan. She died from leukemia brought on by radiation from an atomic bomb.

I pressed against the wall and let people pass, so I could linger in Yad Vashem's Children's Memorial. It was hard to leave and step out into a world where armed conflicts continued. Where children are still being killed.

Will Rachel ever stop weeping for her children? I doubt it. So let us light a candle for all the ones we can name and for the millions whose names we do not know, and resolve to protect our children as best we can. And love each other.

29

A MISSING PIECE

ONCE, DURING A WILD December storm, someone at our house produced a jigsaw puzzle and set it up on a corner table. I don't recall anyone lingering there for more than a few minutes, but almost everyone stopped to fit a piece or two on their way to do something else. Now putting a puzzle together has become a winter tradition for us. Toward the end of the assembly process, it has often been discovered that a piece is missing. It isn't always the manufacturer's fault. The cat could have gotten on the table, or someone may have knocked it off and the vacuum done away with the piece. So we don't have a perfect picture. It is not a big deal to most people. However, finding that something is missing in more significant facets of the winter holidays sometimes really does matter to us.

One Christmas I had trouble with many things. A child needed to go to the hospital several times. Worry about money problems intruded on our time. School activities, both tests and performances, were much more extensive than usual. It was a pretty hectic time without many peaceful moments. Sometime in January it came through to me that there had been almost no carol singing during Christmas. The right combination of people had seldom been together at one time without an agenda. Singing those familiar songs is one of my favorite holiday activities, and I felt the lack of it. These thoughts were with me one morning when I was taking my turn with a toddler who was under the weather.[14] I was sitting in a big rocking chair holding

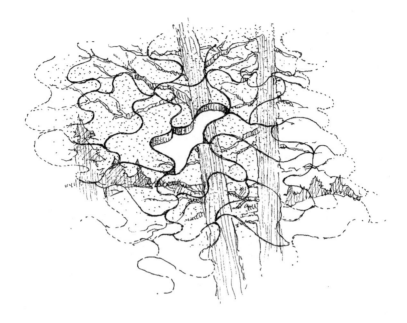

her. We were alone. Why not sing now? So I started singing every carol I could remember. She liked it and we kept it up for a long time, not being reluctant to repeat songs often.

Things that are important to us don't have to be restricted to a certain time frame. An ice dancer, who always is performing in December, makes Christmas cookies in mid-January. Part of one family's custom is to send the two children to their grandmother during the winter school break. The family lives in New Jersey and the grandmother in California. Chanukah is long gone by the time the children arrive, but Chanukah stories are read, and enjoyed, every evening they are with her.

Sometimes that missing piece in our lives cannot be replaced nor the hole filled up. I have never been alone at this time of year as some people I know have been. I know it can be hard for them. However, I have experienced a gap in my intimate circle on more than one occasion. I know this is a common hardship. Some of it is built into life. The first holiday after the death of someone who has been a part of our celebration is difficult, and it is wise to have plans for coping with that. It can also be a shock when that circle around the hearth changes for other reasons. Children who have been essential to past holiday happiness grow up and meet someone with whom they share a new life. That partner will also have a family. Divorce or separation results in stepfamilies, extended families, ex-families. Somebody will be disappointed at Christmas. It takes creative effort to preserve what is important to us about this season. When the issue is missing children or partners, for whatever reason, our expectations must be realistic, and we have to be honest with ourselves and others. One parent I know in a complicated family rearrangement asked her two teenagers, out of desperation, how they wanted to spend the holidays. She was amazed at the wisdom they displayed in making priorities and suggesting plans.

So we have this missing piece in our picture of Christmas. For me it helps to think about it. Sometime in these late December days or nights, it is important to ask myself, "What do I want more of, or less of?" Not that I can necessarily have it, but maybe I can.

We had a situation around New Year's about colored lights on the porch. I had bought some new strings, but the ones we had used for years had been put up again by mistake. They were dinky and faded, and half of them were burned out. During a storm on New Year's Eve the lights gave out completely. It was, for me, a symbol of Christmas being over, and I wasn't ready for that yet. The next morning I produced the sets I had purchased. They had bigger, prettier lights. My suggestion was to put them up. "Put up Christmas lights on New Year's Day?" "In the rain?"

It was an absurd idea to the younger ones, who were ready for Christmas to be over. But when they saw it mattered to me, they reluctantly agreed to help. It didn't take much time, and all conceded they looked nice. I really liked the bright colors on that grey and stormy day. We agreed they would be the last of the decorations to come down.

We started putting things away a few days later. When it came to the porch lights, I said I would like to keep them up. Everyone was horrified. We just don't do things like that. People would think we were too lazy to take them down. For the first few weeks, the kids were seriously embarrassed. Sometime into the rains of February, they redefined my actions as eccentricity, which they could accept but still had to explain to guests. It was always whispered with a slight shrug of the shoulders. Adults found the children's discomfort amusing, and the lights were pretty at night. However, when Easter was in sight, the family was unified in a demand to take them down. We compromised on simply turning them off. Later, when November rolled around, the porch lights went on again, and it has been that way for several years. Now, those lights on the porch are themselves faded and half burned out. What is the point of keeping them up? I don't know exactly, but it supplies something of Christmas that I want to keep with me. As I get older, there are always missing pieces in my Christmas puzzle. The lights on the porch suggest to me that we might take more time to look for the pieces.

It is good to be a little eccentric at this season of the year. Certainly the Bible has Mary and Joseph thinking and acting outside the box. Well, my porch lights are not in their league — but maybe it's a start.

30

THE WINTER WALK

66 $\mathcal{S}$ ILENTLY WE UNLATCH the door, letting the drift fall in, and step abroad to face the cutting air."[15] What is there about walking into the natural world that so strongly attracts writers like Thoreau at this time of year? We will have to open the door and find out.

Even if our walk begins very early in the morning, we are coming into the middle of something. In the city some people have been at work all night. On the dairy farm cows have been milked before dawn. In the fields owls are returning to their dark homes and rabbits are completing their nocturnal adventures. In some regions snow has been falling throughout the night.

Whatever our destination — park, forest, ocean cliff — there will be the sounds and sights of our fellow creatures. This too is sacred. Dogs bark. Cars move down the road. Emergency lights flash. Households wake. Stories are unfolding everywhere we look. The addict blocking the sidewalk or the distracted attendant at the toll booth are not just obstacles to my progress. They are companions on my journey.

When we arrive at a path into a city park or the beginning of a mountain trail, we become mindful of the fresher air. Perhaps it is cold and sharp, coming at us through the branches of leafless trees. What a remarkable world we enter. The songs of birds fill the air, and at our feet are microcosms of living things. The crunch of our shoes reminds us that we too are in a community of existence. There is that line from the first account of the

creation story in the Book of Genesis (1:31), after the sixth day: God saw all that had been made, and indeed it was very good.

Whatever a person's view of the Bible or of biology, the world we experience on a winter walk is "very good" — and we are part of that world. Perhaps when we sense some bond between ourselves, the decaying stump, and the bird standing upon it, there naturally comes a nourishing sorting out of our cares and worries. Maybe it is simply the feeling of being at home.

Some days, plans or hopes for a walk just don't work out. When a sudden storm held me indoors at the farm, I decided to draw on past experiences. Sitting before the fire I thought of the places I had lived and walked. My earliest memory was as a young child walking on a cement seawall between Biloxi and Gulfport, Mississippi. It was a sunny day, and I was walking with my mother. The seawall seemed to separate two worlds. On my left were old houses and trees with long Spanish moss. On my right was the Gulf of Mexico, a few boats and the occasional dolphin popping into sight. The horizon held my attention most as we walked along. I knew about houses and trees, but the sea was a fascinating mystery that expanded my personal horizons.

When I was a young professional, I walked in the forests of Western Oregon. The trees were tall and close together. They formed protective walls. Nothing from the world of my every-day life could be heard or seen. I had to slow down. The forest floor was always damp and soft under my feet. Paths were over-grown. There was a lot of water about. It would cascade down to streams and rivers in beautiful displays. Standing at a waterfall, the thought would often come that while I had been engaged in all manner of hectic pursuits, the water here had been flowing on with powerful tranquility and would continue to do so when I turned my back and walked away. Which was the real world? My office or this mossy spot?

I lived in an Ohio college town during the hard years of civil struggles in the South, in Vietnam, on campus. There was a large nature preserve nearby with inviting paths. I went there many clear and bright winter days. Snow often covered the ground, and the prints of animals and people could be seen in it. There were some enormous oak trees, which I approached with something close to reverence. A creek moved through a glacial crack and spread into a number of cascades. A few were frequently frozen. There was a stone bridge where I always stopped. This was a time when our sense of national innocence was being questioned. Those concerns could never be completely put aside, but it helped to take time out in this undefiled place.

For the past forty years, I have lived in the hills of Northern California. The winter strolls I remember best are along ridges with grasslands falling away on either side. There are a few trees. Some livestock and deer. I can see rivers and lakes in the distance, as well as vineyards and forests. The blue sky is a backdrop for large birds. Turkey vultures often circle lazily high overhead. A Peregrine falcon may sit on a telephone wire surveying the area. There are majestic red-tailed hawks, and sometimes an eagle. Many wonderful sights surround me there, but my eyes keep returning to points on the horizon. The magnificent horizon. If the day is clear, I can sometimes glimpse the ocean to the west, turn, and see snow-capped mountains to the east. The horizon mesmerizes me. In some way the child I was and the man I am in my mid-seventies meet out there where the sky meets the land.

On a winter day, even a short walk can be a pilgrimage. In years past many people visited the Holy Land to recapture something gone missing in their lives. Through the centuries we have come to sense that, in this quest for wholeness, all land may be holy land.

31

PARTING SONGS

I N THE MIDDLE OF WINTER, one icy day is much like another. Why we chose this time to declare a new year I do not know. But we did, and the last day of December is when we say good-bye to the old year. What comes to my mind is champagne glasses, tuxedos, evening gowns, dancing, glittering streamers, crowds, and noise. As I don't often fit into that scene, the alternative has usually been a quiet time at home, reflecting on times past and to come.

In the arbitrary Christian calendar, the last day of the year is the seventh day of Christmas heading toward the feast of the Epiphany on January 6, the day when the Roman church commemorates the visit of the three magi.[16] *Epiphany* is a Greek word for "manifestation," and that is the important point here. There are many ways in which the sacred spirit has been manifested, has broken through, into our history and times. And it doesn't have to happen in a church.

Peter Sellars, the theatrical director and cultural activist, has observed: "Every human being has a spiritual dimension. That's one reason why the arts still exist: to speak to and to nourish the spiritual dimension at a time when people are hungry and yearning and don't go to church. To me the theater is really an important place. Nobody has to be a believer to walk in the door."[17]

Many times I have acted like a believer to walk through a door. Tell me what I have to believe — who I have to be, but just let me in that door! That is the trouble with beliefs; too

often, they are the admission price, the ticket to something —
eternal life or just no longer feeling like a stranger. That is not
an epiphany, a breaking through of the sacred into life.

We learn something of how God has broken through into our
many cultures and differing stories by discovering how we each
actually go about the art of living. As I become more mindful
of the many manifestations, epiphanies, occurring around me
all through the year, I yearn for a time when no one has to be
a believer to walk through any door. There is no better time
for this than the last night of the year. Or any better way to
accomplish it than by rejoicing together in the cultural facets
of our diversity.

The treasured Hindu festival of Diwali occurs in the autumn,
near Halloween. It celebrates the triumph of light over darkness
and how to find the good in all, including our enemies. Diwali
comes to my mind on the last day of the year, partly because it
celebrates the Hindu new year and also because of its Festival
of Lights at sunset. There are thousands of little oil lamps
everywhere. I will never forget seeing kids floating lamps down
a creek in the San Francisco Bay Area. To me, each of us is like
one of those small lamps. The flame of our individual experience
is significant in itself, but it is also part of a spectacular spiritual
display where each light draws attention to all the others.

I have a friend who was, years ago, a Baptist missionary in
Southeast Asia. He told me that his task as a missionary was
to discover how God had already broken through into those
cultures and to bring that light to bear on his own faith.[18]
What can we discover from each other about how to live and
love? A growing number of people are putting aside things that
divide us and concentrating on what light of experience we can
share with each other. Imagine a potluck dinner at which cooks
from differing cultural backgrounds produce dishes associated

with their winter festivals. People from the South would be explaining to the doubtful why you must eat black-eyed peas on this night. We would stumble around other people's cherished dances and songs. And in a quieter moment by the fire, we would share what matters most to each of us and our hopes for the future. There are such gatherings.

Boston has often been a city of friction. In the nineteenth century, the patrician descendants of pilgrims living on Beacon Hill wanted nothing to do with the Irish immigrants flooding the city. In 1974 the Irish of South Boston fought hard to exclude black students from Roxbury. It was a deep conflict. In 1976 a group of Boston artists used their art "as a catalyst to unite the city." First Night was born, and it brought people together — one and a half million each New Year's Eve. There are now over two hundred and fifty performances and exhibitions: fireworks displays, great processions, magnificent ice sculptures, the best in theater, music of all kinds, dance, and film. Two hundred other cities have followed Boston's lead. At these events the excitement comes not from a bottle, but from an outpouring of what is some of the best, and most creative, in the human spirit.

Living in a remote area, I have never been to a First Night. In my home, music marks the evening. Throughout the year, my son David takes note of music that had a special meaning to any of us, or all of us. Shortly after sunset, we sit, or lie, in a room lit only by the fire as he plays recordings. It is an encore performance of the beauty in the year that is ending. After the recordings stop, the music lingers in us for a long time. When it fades, we hear the small sounds of the wind chimes outside, interspersed with silence.

At last there comes the moment to stand up and join our sisters and brothers everywhere in greeting the new year.

32

THE NEXT STEP

T HERE IS A SACREDNESS in every season of the year. During
the winter it is essential to be mindful of that. Winter
has always been a difficult time for many people. The fear and
despair of ancient ancestors who faced this season is still in
our emotional genes somewhere. Plus it is still a hard time.
Birds die in the snow. More elderly people succumb. Death and
suffering go with winter. Although we have learned ways to dis-
tract ourselves from unpleasant realities, they are only temporary
comforts. We all need hope, and that means becoming aware of
the often-unnoticed spiritual aspects of the life around us.

Growing up in the Depression years, I didn't need a book
to tell me life was hard. In those troubled early years, my life
included a small Catholic chapel where life was orderly, peaceful, and secure. I learned to assume that a sacred element would
always be available to me. It need not be in a chapel. It was often
at a hearth-side, in a coffee house, or at a concert hall. It didn't
have to be connected to a place at all. There were friends and
people I loved who provided a welcome transcendence. There
were also strangers and little ordinary things. Somehow, hope
was at hand no matter what I was experiencing. I have often celebrated winter festivals amid personal turbulence. As I mentioned
before, both my father and my mother died, years apart, on the
night before Christmas. My son David's first Christmas was my
mother's last Christmas. Dreams can fade. Disappointments can
overwhelm us. Unforeseen turns in life do happen.

The German artist Albrecht Altdorfer (1480–1538), against all tradition, painted a nativity scene showing a destroyed house, which for all the world resembles a bombed-out dwelling. Jesus, Mary, and Joseph are almost hidden in the shadows of the basement. I think Altdorfer was pointing out that it is in the dark that a divine spark shines best. I first learned about this painting when reading a letter Dietrich Bonhoeffer (1906–1945) wrote to his parents from prison. Bonhoeffer was a German pastor and a member of the Nazi resistance. He was hanged on Hitler's order a few days before Allied forces liberated the prison. In his letter he reflected on Christmas in good times and bad times: "For years you have given us such perfectly lovely Christmases that our grateful recollection of them is strong enough to put a darker one into the background. It is not till such times as these that we realize what it means to possess a past and a spiritual inheritance independent of changes of time and circumstance."[19]

What I take away from that letter is an obligation to make the best of the season in order to help provide a "spiritual inheritance" for ourselves in challenging times and, even more important, for those who will follow us in this story of life.

Sometimes the hope that we all need will be found in a great moment, an epiphany. More often, for me, it is in very common parts of life: a leaf, the stars, raindrops, lights, birds, a train. There is much to help me put my life in perspective within the Christian cultures that have nourished me, but there is also much I have to learn from the experiences of those who were nurtured in other spiritual traditions. Winter weather tends to isolate me, but it also makes me value the very diverse community in which we live. My winter quests ultimately come down to noticing the life experiences of ordinary people. We all encounter joys and sorrows that make each of our stories rich, worth sharing, and helpful.

Occasionally, having things go wrong is more important than having everything work. It took me a number of years to come to value our family's annual struggle with the Christmas tree, or sitting on a dark porch night after night watching a closed lily bud. But those events are now as significant to me as our family drinking Grand Marnier in a child's tea cup on Christmas Eve. Blessed be the imperfect celebration!

My thoughts frequently go to Mary, Joseph, and Jesus. Not only because of my cultural background but because they were a human family. How did they get through that first Christmas? We will never know, but it was undoubtedly more challenging than anything I will ever face. They have, in some way, given to me and to everyone, no matter what spiritual path we walk, "a spiritual inheritance independent of changes of time and circumstance" to be drawn upon at this season of the year. OK, maybe Jesus wasn't born in Bethlehem, but he was born somewhere to a mother who was little more than a child herself. A first birth was a risky matter in those days. Mary might well have died in the process. Joseph was a peasant, which was hard enough. He had no reserves. A birth might ultimately be a joy to him, but he had to go through hell first. I also think often of those other Jewish families throughout history who had their own winter terrors yet produced wonderful stories of encouragement. There is suffering, says the First Noble Truth of Buddhism, and there is also peace to be found under the Bodhi tree. There certainly are times of darkness but, as the small lamps of Diwali remind us, there is always light as well. During Ramadan, our Muslim neighbors recall the desert when they fast during the day. They feast in the evening with renewed awareness of the importance of community. All religious and cultural traditions can teach us facets of the need for love and respect. Or, as the Quakers put it, the need to find something of God in each of us. These are

some of the lessons I want to learn on my meandering winter quests for renewal. My teachers are any people who are using their spiritual inheritance to enrich their daily lives. Jesus was asked, "Who is my neighbor?" He answered with the parable of the Good Samaritan (Luke 10:25–37), which urges us to transcend issues that divide us and simply show compassion to each other. There is no "them," only "us."

Most of us primarily find the sacred within the circle of those we love and find holy ground in our own backyard. Remember the Buddhist monks who go on a three-month retreat during the rainy season? It must be dramatic for them when the retreat ends. For a long time they have been confined to a temple, with strict instructions to destroy no new life. They carefully watch where they put their feet lest they trample a sprout of grass pushing through the cold earth. Then comes the day the retreat ends and they leave. They are given new robes. At the gate they take their final step out of the temple and their first step into a sunny meadow. It is the same step.

In our own backyards, the leaves may be gone and the tree limbs bare. But tiny new buds are beginning to swell. A time will come soon to step between two seasons. Just as with the monks, it is one step. From holy ground to holy ground.

NOTES

1. Talk on December 25, 1977, Thich Nhat Hahn (*www.plumvillage.org/teachings/DharmaTalkTranscripts/Winter*).

2. Robert Duncan, "Childhood's Retreat," *Ground Work: Before the War* (New York: New Directions, 1984), 49, with slightly different editing.

3. Donovan, "The Hurdy Gurdy Man."

4. The direct quotes from *Winterreise* are from the translation of William Mann.

5. Walker Percy, *Love in the Ruins* (New York: Farrar, Straus & Giroux, 1971).

6. Hermann Hesse, *Wandering: Notes and Sketches,* trans. James Wright (New York: Farrar, Straus and Giroux, 1972), 74. All rights reserved, Suhrkamp Verlag, Frankfurt am Main.

7. Paula D'Arcy, *Gift of the Red Bird: A Spiritual Encounter* (New York: Crossroad, 2002), 118–19.

8. Other versions of this event have appeared in various places, including my "Tea Cups and Christmas Angels" in Sharon Bard, Birgit Nielsen, and Clara Rosemarda, eds., *Steeped in the World of Tea* (Northampton, MA: Interlink Books 2005) 167.

9. Tolbert McCarroll, *Childsong, Monksong: A Spiritual Journey* (New York: St. Martin's Press, 1994), 9. This book gives a more complete story of Tina's life, challenges, and impact.

10. Eduardo de Filippo, *Natale in Casa Cupielo,* trans. from Neapolitan-Italian by Anthony Molino with Paul N. Feinberg as *The Nativity Scene: A Play* (Toronto: Guernica Editions, 1997).

11. In recent years Kwanzaa, a week-long cultural festival for African-Americans, has been gaining in popularity. This holiday came out of the frustrations, and the violence, of the black power movements in the 1960s, which was one, often controversial, facet of America's continuing struggle for racial equality and justice. At first, Kwanzaa was a black alternative to Christmas. But it has evolved to become a cultural, rather than a religious or antireligious, event. This has allowed Christians, who are an important part of the African-American community, to adopt it. It is now estimated that about thirty million people worldwide celebrate this festival. One of

Kwanzaa's main attractions for African-American parents is to move beyond the commercial, gift-oriented atmosphere of Christmas and talk about values. The festival goes on for seven nights, and the main event is the evening meal where African clothing is often worn and dances, songs, and symbols are used in an elaborate ritual. Each night one of seven principles is the theme. These are: unity, self-determination, collective work and responsibility, cooperative economics, purpose, creativity, and faith.

12. There really was a Wenceslas (907–935?) who was duke of Bohemia. His grandmother raised him as a Christian. She was strangled by Wenceslas's mother, who assumed the regency much to the relief of the pagan nobles who feared foreign domination. When he was eighteen Wenceslas took over and exiled his mother. Four years later he became a vassal of the German king. A few years later his younger brother Boteslas, with the support of the non-Christian nobles, murdered Wenceslas on his way to church and succeeded him as ruler. Wenceslas is the patron saint of the Czech Republic.

13. The Child Protection division of UNICEF periodically updates information on children who perish in armed conflicts on their website, *www.unicef.org/protection/index_armedconflict.html* and in reports obtainable from UN Publications, 3 United Nations Plaza, New York, NY 10017.

14. I have shared this event from a different perspective in *Childsong, Monksong: A Spiritual Journey* (New York: St. Martin's Press, 1994), 43–44.

15. Henry David Thoreau, "A Winter Walk" *Collected Essays and Poems* (New York: Library of America, 2001), 92. This essay first appeared in 1843.

16. Originally, in the Eastern Church, the Epiphany celebrated the birth of Jesus. Later it became a commemoration of his baptism, which, in three of the gospels, marks the beginning of Jesus' mission. For example, God appears, like a dove, at Jesus' baptism by John and proclaims, "My favor rests on you" (Luke 3:22).

17. *New York Times,* September 25, 2005, AR 35.

18. Paul Clasper, *Eastern Paths and the Christian Way* (Maryknoll, NY: Orbis, 1980). Paul later became a priest in the Anglican community and served as dean of the cathedral in Hong Kong and in numerous academic posts in Asia, the United States, and England.

19. Dietrich Bonhoeffer, *Letters and Papers from Prison,* ed. Eberhard Bethge (New York: Macmillan, 1967), 57.

WITH APPRECIATION

Many people have made this book possible by their encouragement and by sharing their stories. Among those uniquely contributing to the best of what is here are my editor, Roy M. Carlisle, of The Crossroad Publishing Company, and my agent, Edite Kroll. A number of friends critically examined the manuscript and made suggestions, most especially Sharon Bard who read one section a day in the winter before this book was published and contributed her considerable literary skills in suggesting places where the text could be improved. My family was very involved in the process. Marti Aggeler and Julie De Rossi, my lifelong spiritual companions in the Starcross Community, not only went over my work word by word but ensured space in my life for this book to evolve. My children, David, Holly, and Andrew, were not hesitant to react to what I wrote, both thumbs up and thumbs down. They also annually provided the joyful experiences upon which much of this book is based. And, of course, the wonderful and contemplative drawings of Dorothy Beebee bring a welcome light to this winter walk. Any stumbling here is of my own doing. Earlier versions of some aspects of a few pieces in this book appeared in *Sharings,* the Starcross Community newsletter, and other publications including *The Press Democrat.* Some persons' names have been changed. "Emily" in "Plain and Simple" may be an unintentional composite of stories I heard from my Ohio Friend and from Mildred Cowger, a Friend in Oregon who first introduced me to the Quaker path. Sadly, both are now deceased. "Monica," in "Advent Wreath," is an intentional composite of three similar stories. One of the young mothers was living temporarily in New York City, the other two parents lived in the Bay Area.

ACKNOWLEDGMENTS

Grateful acknowledgment is made to the following for permission to reprint previously published material. All quotes from scripture are excerpted from The Jerusalem Bible, copyright © 1966 by Darton, Longman & Todd, Ltd. and Doubleday, a division of Random House, Inc. Reprinted by permission. The lines from Robert Duncan's poem "Childhood's Retreat" © Robert Duncan appear with the cooperation of the Curator of the Robert Duncan Collection at the Poetry/Rare Book Collection at SUNY/Buffalo. The lines from "The Hurdy Gurdy Man" © 1968 Donovan are reprinted by permission of the songwriter. I have been unable to locate William Mann, the translator of the poems by Wilhelm Müller used by Franz Schubert in *Winterreise.* I found them in a concert program with no copyright notice or other clue as to William Mann. The lines from Hermann Hesse, *Wandering: Notes and Sketches,* translated by James Wright, are reprinted by permission of Suhrkamp Verlag, Frankfurt am Main. All rights reserved. The quote from Paula D'Arcy's *Gift of the Red Bird: A Spiritual Encounter* © 1996 Paula D'Arcy is reprinted by permission of The Crossroad Publishing Company. The quote from a letter by Dietrich Bonhoeffer appearing in *Letters and Papers from Prison* © 1967 SCM Press Ltd. is reprinted by permission of SCM-Canterbury Press Ltd.

ABOUT THE AUTHOR

Tolbert McCarroll, better known as "Brother Toby," has lived by Meister Eckhart's adage that what a person acquires in contemplation should be spent in compassion. He is a highly respected spiritual guide for people on many paths and journeys. An award-wining author of nine books, including *Notes from the Song of Life* and *Childsong, Monksong*, he is a founding member of the Starcross Community, a small lay community in the monastic tradition. A former attorney for humanitarian causes, he still frequently ventures forth in response to children in need. The adoptive father of six children, he has established homes for children oppressed by the AIDS pandemic in California, Romania, Uganda and South Africa. He lives at Starcross in Sonoma County, California, where he writes and helps grow olives.

A WORD
FROM THE EDITOR

I have two new heroes in my life this year. One is my older brother, Dick, who now has stepped into the ring four times to battle lymphoma and has taken his knocks and gotten up swinging each time. In the midst of that battle he keeps working out, stays fit, and puts me to shame with his determination. Even now in his early sixties he can leave me in the dust for the first mile of a run. It is deliciously humiliating.

My second hero is Brother Tolbert McCarroll. We had the distinct pleasure of working on a book together a few years ago entitled *Thinking with the Heart.* It was a wonderfully written spiritual testament. But this time around, as we have been working on the book you hold in your hands entitled *A Winter Walk,* which includes provocative and profound seasonal reflections, Brother Toby has been doing the same dance with life that my brother Dick has been doing. Toby is battling his own cancer and even in the midst of it he has written grace-filled reflections, kept up with deadlines that have been daunting, and never wavered in keeping his spirits high. Again, this time with his life, he is writing a spiritual testament, and many lesser men would not have been able to endure this challenge so courageously.

Every day I marvel at this ability of ordinary people to do extraordinary things. But I am wondering if Dick or Toby is really an ordinary person? Probably not. They are extraordinary in that they will not allow themselves to succumb to pity, nor will they allow their circumstances to cast them down into depression. In fact they are often the most alive person in a room!

A few months ago Brother Toby visited me in my former home in the Oakland hills. I am sure at the time the visit had a very important reason for being, but what I remember now is that he was more concerned about all of us than he was about himself. And at the time he was right in the middle of treatments for his cancer, which had to be grueling. But we had a delightful visit, and he and his comrade went on their way. Afterwards I pondered how his whole life had been a preparation for helping others face their mortality and their spirituality. He was also living out that commitment in his Starcross community, in which they adopt children who are suffering from HIV/AIDS. As a community they continually fight for life and maintain a responsible ethic of caring for the least of us.

Over the years Brother Toby has used his felicitous writing to help and guide others and in so doing challenge all of us to live in a world larger than our own petty concerns. My gratitude for who he is grows every time I work on a new essay or reflection because his writing humbly challenges me and each of us to live beyond our individual worlds. In his life and in my brother Dick's life I see "glimpses of the sacred," as Brother Toby calls them, and my life is richer for having seen and experienced those moments.

Roy M. Carlisle
Senior Editor

Of Related Interest

Paula D'Arcy
A NEW SET OF EYES
Encountering the Hidden God

Through a series of meditations and parables, D'Arcy helps readers awaken the mind to the presence of God, free the soul from its cherished idols, and infuse the emotions with joy. By the popular author of *Gift of the Red Bird* and *Song for Sarah*.

0-8245-1930-2, $16.95 hardcover

Henri J. M. Nouwen
ENCOUNTERS WITH MERTON
Spiritual Reflections

Only an artist can truly understand the world of other artists, and only a great spiritual teacher can truly fathom the spiritual depths of other teachers. Nouwen's words bring Merton's vision to life in a way no other book can, while revealing so much of his own vision of the spiritual life.

0-8245-2149-8, $14.95, paperback

crossroad